WHAT IS
DRUG POLICY
FOR?

'An interesting, engaging and accessible book on a topic of huge yet underexamined personal and societal importance.'
David Nutt, Imperial College London

'Professor Buxton takes us on a very genuine and reflective journey of the developments and contradictions of drug policy, navigating the politics and morals of drugs in policy making and its devastating impact on individuals and families. An essential read!'
Karen A. Joe Laidler, University of Hong Kong

'In no health domain is the gap between what policies are and what the evidence says they should be as huge as in drug policies. Julia Buxton is one of the most respected scientists to discuss this.'
Michel Kazatchkine, Special Advisor to the World Health Organization Regional Office for Europe

'A must-read for anyone interested in understanding the irrational and racist origins of drug prohibition. Importantly, Buxton outlines the urgent solutions needed to address the catastrophic harms the system has created.'
Niamh Eastwood, Release

'An urgent rallying cry laying bare the global hypocrisies underlying the local harms of existing drug policies. Buxton equips activists with persuasive weapons to counter punitive models and promote health- and rights-based alternatives.'
Maria-Goretti Ane, consultant in drug policy, harm reduction and human rights

The status quo is broken. The world is grappling with a web of challenges that could threaten our very existence. If we believe in a better world, now is the time to question the purpose behind our actions and those taken in our name.

Enter the What Is It For? series – a bold exploration of the core elements shaping our world, from religion and free speech to animal rights and war. This series cuts through the noise to reveal the true impact of these topics, what they really do and why they matter.

Ditching the usual heated debates and polarizations, this series offers fresh, forward-thinking insights. Leading experts present groundbreaking ideas and point to ways forward for real change, urging us to envision a brighter future.

Each book dives into the history and function of its subject, uncovering its role in society and, crucially, how it can be better.

Series editor: George Miller

Visit **bristoluniversitypress.co.uk/what-is-it-for** to find out more about the series.

Available now

WHAT ARE ANIMAL RIGHTS FOR?
Steve Cooke

WHAT IS COUNTERTERRORISM FOR?
Leonie Jackson

WHAT IS CYBERSECURITY FOR?
Tim Stevens

WHAT IS DRUG POLICY FOR?
Julia Buxton

WHAT IS HISTORY FOR?
Robert Gildea

WHAT IS HUMANISM FOR?
Richard Norman

WHAT IS JOURNALISM FOR?
Jon Allsop

WHAT IS THE MONARCHY FOR?
Laura Clancy

WHAT ARE MUSEUMS FOR?
Jon Sleigh

WHAT ARE THE OLYMPICS FOR?
Jules Boykoff

WHAT IS PHILANTHROPY FOR?
Rhodri Davies

WHAT ARE PRISONS FOR?
Hindpal Singh Bhui

WHAT IS TRUTH FOR?
N.J. Enfield

WHAT IS VEGANISM FOR?
Catherine Oliver

WHAT IS WAR FOR?
Jack McDonald

WHAT IS THE WELFARE STATE FOR?
Paul Spicker

WHAT ARE ZOOS FOR?
Heather Browning and Walter Veit

Forthcoming

WHAT IS ANARCHISM FOR?
Nathan Jun

WHAT IS ANTHROPOLOGY FOR?
Kriti Kapila

WHAT ARE CONSPIRACY THEORIES FOR?
James Fitzgerald

WHAT IS FIFA FOR?
Alan Tomlinson

WHAT IS FREE SPEECH FOR?
Gavan Titley

WHAT IS IMMIGRATION POLICY FOR?
Madeleine Sumption

WHAT IS INTERNATIONAL DEVELOPMENT FOR?
Andrea Cornwall

WHAT ARE MARKETS FOR?
Phillip Roscoe

WHAT IS MUSIC FOR?
Fleur Brouwer

WHAT	**ARE NUCLEAR WEAPONS FOR?**
	Patricia Shamai
WHAT	**ARE THE POLICE FOR?**
	Ben Bradford
WHAT	**IS RELIGION FOR?**
	Malise Ruthven
WHAT	**IS RESILIENCE FOR?**
	Hamideh Mahdiani
WHAT	**IS SPACE EXPLORATION FOR?**
	Tony Milligan and Koji Tachibana
WHAT	**ARE STATUES FOR?**
	Milly Williamson

JULIA BUXTON is Professor of Justice at Liverpool John Moores University. She was previously British Academy Global Professor in Criminology at the University of Manchester, and Professor and Acting Dean of School at Central European University in Budapest, Hungary. She has taught and trained on drug histories and enforcement impacts for 25 years, running courses for students, non-governmental organizations (NGOs), the armed forces and policy officials. Julia has served on the advisory and executive boards of several drug policy-related grant bodies, academic projects and NGOs, currently the Eurasian Harm Reduction Association. A specialist on the development and gendered impacts of drug policy, she is a Latin Americanist by background, with a PhD researched in Venezuela (1994–98).

WHAT IS DRUG POLICY FOR?

JULIA BUXTON

First published in Great Britain in 2025 by

Bristol University Press
University of Bristol
1–9 Old Park Hill
Bristol
BS2 8BB
UK
t: +44 (0)117 374 6645
e: bup-info@bristol.ac.uk

Details of international sales and distribution partners are available at
bristoluniversitypress.co.uk

© Julia Buxton 2025

British Library Cataloguing in Publication Data
A catalogue record for this book is available from the British Library

ISBN 978-1-5292-4144-0 paperback
ISBN 978-1-5292-4145-7 ePub
ISBN 978-1-5292-4146-4 ePdf

The right of Julia Buxton to be identified as author of this work has been asserted
by her in accordance with the Copyright, Designs and Patents Act 1988.

All rights reserved: no part of this publication may be reproduced, stored in
a retrieval system, or transmitted in any form or by any means, electronic,
mechanical, photocopying, recording, or otherwise without the prior permission of
Bristol University Press.

Every reasonable effort has been made to obtain permission to reproduce
copyrighted material. If, however, anyone knows of an oversight, please contact
the publisher.

The statements and opinions contained within this publication are solely those of the
author and not of the University of Bristol or Bristol University Press. The University
of Bristol and Bristol University Press disclaim responsibility for any injury to
persons or property resulting from any material published in this publication.

Bristol University Press works to counter discrimination on grounds of gender,
race, disability, age and sexuality.

Cover design: Tom Appshaw

This book is dedicated to the memory of
Professor David Bewley-Taylor and his
extraordinary contribution to drug policy
scholarship and drug policy change.

CONTENTS

List of Tables and Boxes		xiv
Acknowledgements		xv
Introduction		1
1	**Drug Criminalization: Is it Working?**	6
2	**Building an International Drug Prohibition**	34
3	**The Persistence of the Drug User**	67
4	**The Problem of Endless Supply**	100
5	**What Chance of Drug Policy Reform?**	132
Further Reading		166
Index		180

LIST OF TABLES AND BOXES

Tables

5.1	Comparative threshold quantities for personal use possession	140

Boxes

1.1	Rose, I	18
1.2	Suzanne, I	19
2.1	Scotland's drug-related deaths	38
2.2	Drug scheduling in the UK	40
3.1	Crack cocaine in the US	77
3.2	Synthetic drugs, the 'Angels'	79
3.3	Gender in drug policy	90
3.4	Rose, II	94
3.5	Happy, I	96
3.6	Suzanne, II	98
4.1	Fumigation costs	107
4.2	Alternative development: the Thailand model	109
4.3	A coca memory	116
4.4	The value of cocaine	121
5.1	Double standards and doublespeak	144
5.2	Happy, II	154
5.3	Psychedelic renaissance	162

ACKNOWLEDGEMENTS

Enormous thanks to Niamh Finucane for keeping the lights on, the children fed and the coffee on tap while I oscillated between purdah and procrastination.

INTRODUCTION

This short book considers the global strategy of criminalizing the unauthorized trade in, and use of, over three hundred mind- and mood-altering plants and synthetic drugs. It explores the roots of this approach, how it became global orthodoxy and how criminalization 'performs' and enables policy objectives to be met – or not.

The goal of drug policy is set out in the 1961 United Nations (UN) Single Convention on Narcotic Drugs: to end the 'serious evil' of addiction. This is to be achieved by preventing public access to dangerous substances while at the same time ensuring adequate provision of these 'narcotics' to meet medical and scientific requirements. These twin elements encapsulate the 'dual use dilemma' that has confronted drug policy makers for the past 150 years. Some of these substances, especially opiates such as morphine and codeine from the opium poppy, are extraordinarily effective for pain management, as the Greek physician Hippocrates pointed out back in 400 BCE. These substances are 'indispensable for the relief of pain and suffering', as the preamble to the 1961 Single Convention puts it. The problem is that the medical virtue of being in a pain-free 'altered state' can also become a vice.

The approach agreed by governments is to protect virtue (medical use) and to forcefully step in to prevent vice ('recreational' use). Activity involving the banned substances listed in the 1961 and follow-up 1971 and 1988 UN drug treaties is criminalized. Exceptionally, and only with high-level government authorization, these prohibited plants and synthetic drugs may be cultivated, manufactured, transported, distributed and used for medical and scientific purposes.

You may already have a view as to how drug criminalization has performed in the six decades since the UN Single Convention was adopted. People tend to be less familiar with drug control performance in relation to the second element of policy: access to essential medicines. This is where my interest in the drug world came in.

In 1997, my family suffered a devastating loss. She was intelligent, witty, and the mother to a one-year-old. Her diagnosis involved too few trips for palliative advice. To escape the desperate sadness of the treatment wards and corridors, I took to the 'Garden of Reflection', where I met another distressed soul. She had travelled with her brother thousands of miles to the UK so he could be a patient at this specialist London hospital. The transcontinental journey had bankrupted the family, but they did not want him to die in agony. He had terminal brain cancer. Paracetamol was the strongest analgesic that was available in the hospitals where she came from.

She told me that back home, her parents had begged the best-paid oncologist in the country for morphine prescription for their dying son. The oncologist refused, fretting that the brother would become addicted to the opiate. When the parents protested that their son had just a month to live, the oncologist revealed that even if he was inclined to prescribe this pain-relieving drug, it was simply unavailable nationally. The government did not import stocks of morphine.

The sister hatched a desperate plan to obtain opiates from a different source: street heroin. She had no idea where to get it or what it looked like, and faced the prospect of years in prison if caught by police. With three kids, that was a gamble, so her parents sold the family home to fund this trip to Britain and end-of-life care for their son. The conversation was unfathomable to me. What a cruel and backward country she came from.

I returned home to the *Local Gazette* and another breathless front-page report of yet another drug raid (for heroin) on the house around the corner that had been raided the month before. I went to skulk on the internet. Could my new acquaintance's tale possibly be true? It was 1997. The internet took a long time to connect. Finally, an article that laid out the shocking details. It turned out the UK was an exception rather than the rule.

Over 90 per cent of the global population had little to zero access to morphine, a World Health Organization essential medicine since 1977. Imagine compound fractures, surgery, childbirth or the crushing tumours of cancer and HIV with no pain relief. In the poorest countries there was also unlikely to be a hospital or specialist treatment within easy reach and as disease and tumours progressed. Just a terrible death. Without pain relief.

It was depressing stuff. The next link optimistically had the words 'hope' and 'dignity.' It was an extraordinary piece about a Liverpool doctor, Anne Merriman, pioneering local manufacture of cheap morphine solution and hospice care for rural communities in Uganda ravaged by HIV. It gave me the strength to stay on the internet.

UN drug control bodies had authorized 1,200 metric tonnes of legal opium production that year to ensure global access to drugs 'indispensable for the relief of pain and suffering'. So, what had happened to these opiate medications? They were hoovered up by a handful of countries: around 70 per cent went to the US, Australia, Canada and the UK.

We were hearing a lot about the Afghan Taliban in 1997, including in the *Local Gazette*. We were going to be hearing a whole lot more after the attacks on the US on 9/11 (11 September 2001) and the US-led invasion of Afghanistan the following month. In 1997 the Taliban were in the news for military advances against the US-backed Northern Alliance in Afghanistan's protracted violent conflict. US authorities claimed the Taliban had reversed a strict ban on growing and taxing opium poppy in areas under their control. They were now flush with opium revenues. Where did this Afghan opium fit in with urgent and unmet global demand for essential opioid medicines? It didn't.

INTRODUCTION

The licensed commercial cultivation of opium poppy was dominated by two countries: the UK and Australia. France, Turkey and India also contributed to the 1,200 metric tonnes of legal production. At the same time, Afghanistan, alongside Laos and Myanmar, was illicitly producing around 4,300 metric tonnes, some of which was routinely available in the house around the corner that preoccupied the *Local Gazette*. It seemed that whoever oversaw opiate policy might want to rethink. The system seemed to be failing *both* in preventing access to 'narcotics' *and* in ensuring availability of essential medicines.

Over the next decades of my academic research career, the drug policy problem revealed itself to be far larger than the management of opiates, far more difficult to reform than expected, and with an outlook far more worrying than you might have imagined when you started this book. I would like to thank the British Academy Global Professorships Programme and the Open Society Foundations Global Drug Policy Program for the funding that has enabled me to teach, research and network with stakeholders in drug policy from across the world. Those interviews, conferences and workshops inform the chapters ahead.

1
DRUG CRIMINALIZATION: IS IT WORKING?

Substances that alter our brain and mental processes are ubiquitous. Wherever you are reading this, you are almost certain to be within metres of a psychoactive substance. Perhaps a caffeine-laden coffee, energy drink or gin? You might shortly be reaching for a cigarette, nicotine-infused vape, or analgesic relief in the form of over-the-counter painkilling tablets. You might be one of the 8.6 million people in the UK or 45 million in the US prescribed anti-depressant or anti-anxiety medications, a subset of the psychoactives referred to as 'psychotropics'. It's less likely that you are smoking a joint. (If you are, we'll check back later to see if you are still with us.)

Our lives are structured around routines, social interactions and ceremonies in which our behaviour and mood are changed by pills, powders, puffs and shots. Adverts for psychoactive products promising alertness, energy, pleasure or relief are pervasive. These legal stimulants and depressants come with risks.

The most immediate harms are to the user and include dependence, insomnia, hypertension and cancer. There are also indirect harms caused to others, for example, the 1.3 million annual deaths linked to second-hand tobacco smoke puffed by the world's 1.3 billion smokers, seven million of whom will suffer premature, smoking-related death each year. A further 2.6 million annual deaths globally are linked to alcohol, with 800,000 people suffering the indirect impacts of alcohol-related public and domestic violence.

Substance-use risks are gendered, impacting men and women differently. For reasons of biology and sociology, men and boys disproportionately use and misuse alcohol and tobacco and suffer a higher proportion of direct harms. Women and girls are more likely to be collateral damage, the victims of male substance use.

Female smoking and alcohol consumption are heavily stigmatized in most countries, leading to lower use and the exclusion of women from public rituals of intoxication. Women do not abjure psychoactive substance use: their patterns of consumption are typically private, alone and for self-medication. Men out-smoke and out-drink women, but more women use anti-depressant, anti-anxiety and pain medication than men.

The struggle for our virtue: temperance or prohibition

Palpitating coffee 'addicts' usually baulk at the suggestion that their habit is comparable to alcohol dependence or (getting ahead of ourselves) cocaine. But the effects of excessive caffeine intake are on a spectrum of substance-related risks and harms. These have differential impacts, not only between men and women but also, for example, between the old and the young, the experienced consumer and the novice. There are two traditional interventions to protect us from our worse, naïve, over-indulgent selves: regulation, through which authorities try to make consumption safer and more moderate; and complete bans.

The route of an enforced ban, or 'prohibition', has been popular with religions. The world's major faiths proscribe alcohol drinking as immoral, viewing inebriation as an impediment to wellbeing, mindfulness and good ethical judgement. Consumer prohibitions have included coffee. The 'black gold' from Ethiopia and Yemen associated with raucous behaviour in coffee shops led to a ban in Mecca in 1511 and in the Ottoman Empire in 1633.

The Roman Catholic church has also issued consumer prohibitions among many other prohibitions. A 1590 decree of Pope Urban VII banned the indecorum of smoking tobacco in and around places of worship. There were smoking bans in European towns such as Berlin, Szczecin, Stockholm and Kaliningrad in the eighteenth century, but motivated by fire risk in dense timber housing, not by a concern with saving souls or lungs.

The modern centralized state and empire did share the anxiety of the minbar and pulpit with intoxication, but generally veered away from prohibition. By the early 1900s, the US and European governments and colonial administrations acknowledged a role for the state in limiting injury caused to citizens and imperial subjects by the unregulated consumption of harmful plants, brews, tonics and potions. The religious language of moral failing persisted but was absorbed into a regulatory narrative that overlaid spiritual judgement with new political and social concerns that were generated by industrialization, urbanization and immigration.

The regulatory impulse: cigarettes and alcohol

Public health, consumer protection and, in the US, social hygiene ideas about the role of the state in preventing disease and promoting good health were influential in the second half of the nineteenth century. They encouraged governments to assume responsibility for managing intoxicants and other consumer items, setting rules about when, where and how these products could be bought, in what quantities and by whom. New laws such as the 1868 Pharmacy Act and the 1893 Sale of Goods Act in the UK and the 1906 Pure Food and Drug Act in the US required content labelling and quality controls to prevent accidental poisoning, counterfeiting, adulteration and underweight goods.

Libertarian critics rejected these interventions as heavy handed, arguing that they undermined free trade, individual choice and entrepreneurialism. There was also hostility from the emerging pharmaceutical sector in Europe and North America that lobbied against regulatory interference in revolutionary new chemistry and medicines.

Objections to limited opening hours, age restrictions and content regulations were marginalized by a confluence of interests supportive of regulation: business owners wanted a productive labour force, churches aspired to temperate congregations, and new professional lobbies such as the British Royal Pharmaceutical Society, founded in 1841, wanted qualified medical experts to arbitrate the prescription and marketing of new medicines and remedies.

Over the decades, this coalition of religious, business, medical and party-political stakeholders remained relatively unchanged, embedding regulation as the principal model for managing consumers' substance risks.

A handful of countries, including Iceland and the US (to which we will return), some states in India, and territories of First Nations people in Canada and Australia, have experimented with contemporary alcohol bans. In 2022 New Zealand hesitantly went for a tobacco ban for future generations (born after 2009). The legislation was reversed the following year, as were alcohol bans in Iceland (1989) and the US (1933).

The prohibition of in-demand substances is difficult to enforce. They create a supply gap that is quickly filled by black markets of substitute goods provided for criminal profit. Transnational corporate power is another consideration for contemporary governments navigating regulation. In 2010, tobacco company Philip Morris International sued Uruguay over new requirements for cigarette packaging. The case went to the International Centre for Settlement of Investment Disputes (ICSID) in Washington DC. The body found in favour of Uruguay, but the victory showed the aggressiveness of the tobacco lobby.

Most commonly, then, we live with warnings and recommendations rather than unenforceable bans and overzealous restrictions. The state relies on our common sense not to tip over the recommended 400 mg of caffeine per day (200 mg for pregnant women), and there is no state surveillance of our Americano or vodka purchases.

Governments globally differ on the robustness of restrictions; nevertheless, there is acknowledgement of the right of citizens to the highest attainable standards of physical and mental health as set out in legal instruments such as the 1948 UN Universal Declaration on Human Rights and the 1966 International Covenant on Economic, Social and Cultural Rights.

A variety of tools encourage us to moderate, if not reduce to zero, our reliance on substances to get us through life pain-free and alert. Public education and prevention campaigns that target vulnerable users such as schoolchildren and pregnant women do have a good record of reducing consumption and related harms if they are maintained over the long term and well-resourced, and provide support to those with a dependence issues. For example, in Uruguay, a package of measures including outdoor smoking restrictions and graphic warnings on packaging (outraging Philip Morris all the way to the ICSID) contributed to a fall in smoking from 35 per cent of the adult population in 2005 to 20 per cent by 2024.

Financial penalties are another mechanism to push us along the road to temperance. Nothing attracts the attention and alters the behaviour of a consumer like a price increase. Taxes on cigarettes, minimum pricing on alcohol and safe disposal levies – for example on vapes – can push down consumption. But it is a difficult balance to achieve. Overinflated costs can galvanize business protests and black markets. It can take years, maybe decades, to alter public perceptions and social norms about risky consumption habits. The best hope for the policy maker is that attitudinal change will occur across generations, as traditional users and old views fade away and new generations look back in horror on the old habits and social practices of their elders.

Criminalization and the management of narcotic drug markets

Absolutely none of the above applies to hundreds of other mind- and mood-altering substances, including the plants and shrubs cannabis, coca and the opium poppy; and their alkaloid derivatives cocaine and crack cocaine from coca, the opiates morphine and heroin from opium, and ephedrine from the ephedra plant, which is used in the manufacture of methamphetamine.

A galaxy of 'man-made' drugs also fall into this distinct class of substances. These include amphetamine-type substances (ATS) such as amphetamine and methamphetamine; empathogens and hallucinogens such as MDMA and LSD; dissociative drugs such as ketamine; novel synthetic opioids (NSOs) such as fentanyl and tramadol; and unauthorized anti-depressant and anti-anxiety drugs such as benzodiazepines and 'street drugs', which are unregulated copies of these pharmaceutical medications.

Most of these substances have been discarded from clinical research or prescription following disappointing trial results or negative side-effects. For example, 3,4-Methylenedioxymethamphetamine, first synthesized by Merck in 1912 as a blood-clotting agent but discontinued for clinical practice after the development of a more effective drug, was reinvented as the club drug Ecstasy/MDMA 80 years later.

National systems of licensing and consumer protection that are feasible for tobacco and alcohol are abjured for this special class of substances. Governments globally have rejected regulation in favour of a co-ordinated international ban. As discussed in the next chapter, the UN drug treaties that structure global agreement go so far as recommending regimes of prosecution and punishment of those who defy the prohibition. The gravity of offence is determined by the classification of substances in the UN treaties. Cannabis, heroin, opium, methadone, cocaine and the coca leaf are all classed under Schedule I (or Class A under the UK system) for the most dangerous substances, those determined to have a high risk of addiction and no therapeutic or scientific value. Activities such as cultivation, manufacture, transportation, distribution and possession of Schedule I substances attract the most severe penalties.

People in illicit drug markets are not gently nudged into different behaviours. They are stigmatized and punished with draconian sentences, including mandatory minimum jail terms, arbitrary detention, and deprivation of other liberties, rights and freedoms. Involvement in this illicit market is not only free of consumer or legal protections, but human rights also go out of the window.

The coercive state and enforcement violence

Thirty-five countries retain the death penalty for drug-related offences. According to the non-government agency (NGO) Harm Reduction International, a record 467 people were executed in 2023 under national drug laws, including in Iran, Saudi Arabia, China, Kuwait, Vietnam and Singapore. Human rights groups raised major concerns over access to justice, due process, corruption, and fabricated charges against migrant workers and political regime opponents.

In the Philippines, President Rodrigo Duterte went for a strategy of extrajudicial execution, urging supporters to shoot drug sellers 'and I'll give you a medal'. He outlined: 'If you lose your job, I will give you one. Kill all the drug addicts.' By January 2018, around 12,000 people had been murdered by lynch mobs and death squads. The horror of Duterte's response is extreme, but lethal enforcement of prohibition has parallels elsewhere. Prime minister Sheikh Hasina unleashed a murderous war on drugs in Bangladesh in 2018, and in Thailand there were 2,800 extrajudicial killings in the 2003 'drug war' of former prime minister and former owner of Manchester City Football Club, Thaksin Shinawatra.

These violent responses are at one end of a spectrum of coercive measures to stamp out illicit drug markets that have intensified over the decades of the global narcotics ban. The world prison population has increased by around 25 per cent between 2000 and 2023, mainly due to pre-trial detentions and sentencing for low-level, non-violent drug (possession) offences. There is an accumulation of evidence of significant racial disparities in drug-related policing and sentencing processes, and law enforcement targeting of minority and vulnerable communities. According to a 2024 report by the Global Commission on Drug Policy (GCDP) on HIV, hepatitis and drug policy reform, a fifth of the roughly eleven million prisoners worldwide are incarcerated on drug-related charges. Over 1.7 million people were convicted for offences related to drug trafficking. An additional half a million people are involuntarily held in drug detention centres, mainly in Southeast Asian countries including Cambodia, Vietnam, Laos and China.

Rising levels of drug-related pre-trial detention and incarceration have created serious problems of prison overcrowding. Prison systems in more than

120 countries were operating at over 100 per cent capacity, with 15 exceeding 250 per cent, according to a 2024 report by GCDP. There are problematic geographical hotspots.

In Southeast Asia, Philippine prisons were operating at 436 per cent capacity (2018), at 202 per cent in Indonesia and at 145 per cent in Thailand. In South and Central America, prison occupancy levels in El Salvador and Guatemala were at 333 per cent capacity, at 254 per cent in Bolivia, and 165 per cent in Brazil.

There has been a vertiginous increase in the numbers of women jailed on drugs charges (often with their babies) in regional contexts such as Southeast and Central Asia and the Americas (North, Central and South). In 2018, the United Nations Office on Drugs and Crime (UNODC) reported a total population of 714,000 women prisoners worldwide, 35 per cent of whom were incarcerated for drug-related offences, contrasting with 19 per cent of the male prison population.

This trend of female overincarceration started in the US, where the number of women in prison between 1980 and 2019 escalated from 26,378 to 222,455. In England and Wales, the proportion of women prisoners detained for drug offences increased from 29 per cent to 37 per cent between 1990 and 2000. This was linked to the use of determinate and mandatory minimum sentencing that cannot be appealed or revised, and in which the context of the offence and mitigating factors is not considered. There was a 52 per cent increase in numbers of female prisoners in South America between 2000 and 2015, and a third of female prisoners in Azerbaijan, Kyrgyzstan and Russia were convicted of drug-related offences, rising to 70 per cent in Tajikistan (bordering Afghanistan).

This trend went against the 1990 UN Standard Minimum Rules for Non-custodial Measures (known as the 'Tokyo Rules') that emphasize alternatives to custodial sentences, such as diversion, probation, treatment, community sanctions and community service orders, and the 2010 UN Rules for the Treatment of Women Prisoners and Non-custodial Measures for Women Offenders (or 'Bangkok Rules'). These rules require mitigating factors to be considered when sentencing women (Rule 61) and emphasize non-custodial sentences for pregnant women and women with dependent children (Rule 64) and the provision of gender-sensitive correctional facilities. Women of colour, migrant women and poor women are over-represented in the expanding women's global prison population.

The numbers of men, women and juveniles detained on drugs charges adds to the swelling global population of prisoners convicted of other non-drug related forms of criminal activity. This includes 'minor' offences such as sex work and theft to support a substance use disorder (SUD). An estimated one in three prisoners use drugs during their confinement.

By contrast with the clinical support and substitution therapies available to users under the regulation model – think nicotine patches, alcohol-free booze and counselling – a slog through the annual reports of Harm Reduction International presents a dismal global picture for all people who want to stop using drugs, or who simply want to use safely. Appropriate and accessible drug treatment, testing, and harm reduction services are in short supply in most countries and in high-risk settings such as prisons. Where these do exist, they are typically underfunded and subject to political contestation: initiatives such as needle exchanges, opiate substitution therapies (such as prescription methadone) and overdose reversal kits (Nalaxone/Narcon) are construed by critics as *enabling* drug use.

> **Box 1.1: Rose, I**
>
> In 2020, I interviewed Rose for an edited collection (published by Emerald later that year) that explored *The Impact of Global Drug Policy on Women*. Rose lost her two sons, Roland and Jake, to drug overdoses. She told me about the struggle to get access to treatment and support, and the isolating impacts of addiction on the family:
>
>> The dreadful thing is the stigma because no matter how bad I was feeling there was nobody I could talk to. I did not dare reveal it to my friends and neighbours, to people at work and to my parents. So some days I would wake up – if I had managed to sleep – and I just wanted to burst into tears.

Seeking family, clinical or employer support may lead to a police or child services referral, the removal of any children or redundancy. In US states such as Arizona and Kentucky pregnant women who test positive for banned substances forfeit parental rights and custody of their newborn, while in Alabama, South Carolina and Tennessee they face charges of child abuse. These statistics are cited by police and political authorities as policy and enforcement success.

> **Box 1.2: Suzanne, I**
>
> In 2020, I also interviewed Suzanne:
>
> > Women have gone in, asked for help and because they have done that social services have been involved and their children taken away, but all they wanted was help. I was using problematically but managing to hold it together – that is how it is for many women, they have their kids and that is enabling them to hold it together. When social services get involved and take the children away that is the last straw. People say, if your children have been taken away then why not get your act together? They just don't understand this illness. I know too many women who have taken their own lives because of it. And that is criminal. And where are the kids now – the next generation of traumatized kids?

Measure what you treasure: evaluating the success of criminalization strategy

Criminalization has determined that progress towards the global goal of preventing unauthorized public access to drugs is measured by law enforcement-based indicators. This makes for vastly different metrics and strategic priorities than, say, a public health led response. The UN requires all countries to participate in a reporting process called the Annual Report Questionnaire (ARQ). This data-driven exercise informs the UNODC's annual World Drug Report. The ARQ captures volumes and type of drugs seized, plants eradicated by enforcement agencies, and numbers of people arrested and prosecuted for drug-related offences. On paper, and as demonstrated by the increase in executions, incarcerations and detentions, enforcement is looking robust – if not outrageously overzealous.

On the supply side of illicit markets, drug seizures, like drug prosecutions, are at record levels in countries worldwide. In 2022 authorities in Saudi Arabia intercepted the largest-ever consignment of amphetamine tablets (46 million) trafficked into the Kingdom, while in Europe, authorities in Belgium seized a record 100 metric tonnes of cocaine at Antwerp port. The previous year saw record methamphetamine hauls (172 metric tonnes) in East and Southeast Asia, and Cape Verde, Senegal and Benin in West Africa reported record cocaine seizures of 57 metric tonnes. Enforcement co-operation between countries is robust, and as discussed in Chapter 4, record volumes of drug seizures are paralleled by record levels of drug crop eradication in cultivating countries such as Colombia, Peru and Bolivia (coca).

Given robust enforcement on *both* the demand *and* the supply side of illicit drug markets, and the severity of punishment for drug-related offences, it might be expected the illicit market would be contracting. This is not the case. It is booming.

Drug demand under criminalization: record highs

Drug use data is unreliable. UN and national figures are widely thought to underestimate the scale of illicit drug markets and substance use. Criminalization makes it difficult to accurately capture drug user numbers and behaviours, the context and frequency of use, and the types and combinations of substances that are consumed. Prohibition strategies and draconian punishment regimes create hidden and stigmatized populations. People are reluctant to disclose criminal activity, and researchers face legal, ethical and security hazards collecting information. Many countries simply lack the public health staff to conduct surveys and instead rely on estimates of user numbers.

There are acknowledged limitations with UNODC and national drug statistics. Nevertheless, a contemporary snapshot of the figures for drug consumption, cultivation and manufacture at the start of the 2020s enables us to better evaluate the performance of the criminalization regime six decades into a global prohibition.

The data, based on national reporting to UN drug control bodies in the ARQ, show a dense and dynamic illicit sector and millions of undeterred users. As outlined by Ghada Waly, Executive Director of the UNODC, in her introduction to the 2020 *World Drug Report*, 'More people are using drugs, and there are more drugs, and more types of drugs, than ever.' The 2023 edition cited a figure of 300 million people in a global population of eight billion using a controlled substance in 2021 – 25 per cent more than a decade earlier. This consumer market growth is attributed to factors such as increased supply and availability, agile drug trafficking networks, open borders and improved consumer spending power.

The number of people using drugs is projected to rise a further 11 per cent by 2030. Africa is expected to see a 40 per cent increase as the continent becomes more deeply embedded in transnational routes moving cocaine from the West (Latin America) and opiates and synthetics from the East (Asia), and due to the growth of domestic synthetic drug manufacture capacity within African countries.

Cannabis

UNODC reporting shows cannabis is universally popular, despite a century-long international campaign to eliminate the plant led by the US federal government. Cannabis herb (grass) and resin (hash) are the most widely consumed controlled substances. Although medical and adult recreational cannabis markets have been decriminalized in some jurisdictions (see Chapter 5), criminalization prevails in most countries.

There are an estimated two hundred million cannabis users, predominantly men, who outnumber women users at a ratio of around 4 to 1. The highest rates of illicit cannabis use (at least a tenth of the adult population) are found in North America, Australia, and West and Central Africa. In Europe, around 8 per cent of the adult population are regular cannabis users, but as with other regions (for example South America), there are national variations. Cannabis is more commonly consumed in Czechia, France, Germany, Spain and the UK in the European context. By contrast, Hungary, Bulgaria and Portugal have low levels of cannabis use.

In South America, the Southern cone countries of Chile, Argentina and Uruguay sit at the high end of the prevalence spectrum, while Peru, Ecuador and Bolivia sit at the opposite end, with low levels of cannabis consumption. These divergences are explained by factors such as market access, availability and price of cannabis products, and distinct norms and traditions of cannabis use, for example in spiritual practice, popular culture and traditional medicine.

Opioids

Opioids (which include organic opium poppy derivatives such as morphine, heroin and codeine – opiates – *and* synthetics such as fentanyl) are the second most consumed controlled substance category, with 62 million users (2021). North America, Australia and

New Zealand have user rates above the global average of 1.2 per cent. Despite a low prevalence of just 2 per cent, the populous region of South Asia accounts for around a third of opioid users.

Fentanyl and its many analogues (fentalogs) are the most reported substances among the 9.9 million people using non-medical prescription opioids in the US, and the principal cause of overdose and drug-related deaths in the country. The toll of the US drug crisis is staggering. There were just short of 40,000 deaths in 2010. This spiralled to over 93,000 a decade later. The US Centers for Disease Control estimate nearly 70,000 of 2020 overdose deaths were linked to opioids.

The dire trajectory continued into the 2020s, with 105,007 deaths in 2023, equivalent to 31.3 per 100,000 of the US population. Canada is also experiencing a seemingly uncontainable opiate crisis that has been accelerated by fentanyl. The government declared a public health emergency in 2016, but the death toll continued to rise. In British Columbia, the epicentre of overdose deaths, there were 2,511 fatalities in 2023. This is a far lower figure in comparison to the US but adjusted for population size it represents 45.7 per 100,000 residents of the province. In North, Central and West Africa, national authorities report tramadol to be the primary synthetic opioid of misuse.

Amphetamine Type Substances

There are an estimated thirty million users of ATS, another type of synthetic stimulant drug. The highest per capita consumption rates for ATS such as methamphetamine (meth) and amphetamine are in North America, Australia and New Zealand. In terms of user numbers, the populous countries of Southeast Asia account for half of global consumers. The UNODC notes a 'strong shift' in Southeast Asia away from heroin to cheaper methamphetamine: 'With the exception of Viet Nam, all the thirteen countries in the region reported methamphetamine as their primary drug of concern in 2018 [...] a decade ago only five countries reported that to be the case.'

As discussed in Chapter 4, the expansion of the Southeast Asian meth market can in part be explained as 'blowback': the unintended, negative outcome of strategies to eradicate opium poppy cultivation in countries such as Myanmar. Progress in containing illicit plant farming and related criminal interests is offset by a shift into methamphetamine (known locally as *yaba*) manufacture. The drug is available for local users in Myanmar but is principally for export. Lucrative markets in China, Thailand, Bangladesh, Indonesia, the Philippines, South Korea, Australia and New Zealand have an estimated annual value of up to US$60 billion.

Methamphetamine is also seen by authorities in Africa as a ballooning problem. Paralleling earlier trends in North America, Australasia and Southeast Asia, the use of heroin and other opioids is being overtaken by cheap methamphetamine. Jason Eligh of the Global Initiative against Transnational Organized Crime has researched 'footholds' in eSwatini, Lesotho, Botswana,

Mozambique, Malawi, Zambia, Zimbabwe, Uganda and Kenya for methamphetamine manufactured in Nigeria and South Africa.

In Europe, amphetamine is more widely consumed than methamphetamine. This reflects a long-standing division of ATS markets: meth to the east, amphetamine to the west. Poland, Germany and the Netherlands have among the highest rates of amphetamine use. MDMA is another synthetic that has endured as a popular nightlife drug in Europe, North America and Australasia, with 20.5 million users.

Novel Psychoactive Substances

A key problem for international drug control is keeping ahead of – or at least in step with – innovations in illicit drug chemistry. This has proved difficult in a global system that has been focused on plant-based substances (cocaine, heroin and cannabis) for over a century, and for bureaucratic international institutions that move slowly. The architects of international drug control paid little attention to synthetic drugs. Regulation and management were effectively devolved to national authorities. The 1971 UN Convention on Psychotropic Substances did step up oversight of the synthetic drug sector but in the contemporary period, synthetic innovation has accelerated beyond the capacity for system response. This has been facilitated by the internet as a forum for the exchange of knowledge and purchase of the precursor chemicals that are required for drug synthesis, for example ephedrine and pseudoephedrine used to make methamphetamine, acetic anhydride in the manufacture of heroin, and piperonal and safrole for Ecstasy. A key challenge for authorities is that these chemicals are commonly used in the legitimate chemical industry, for the manufacture of cleaning products, pesticides, lubricants and cosmetics.

The UN and national drug control authorities have been left far behind, unable to contain a proliferation of new and dangerous synthetic drugs that are legal by default because of the slowness of the treaty system in identifying new drug threats. Novel Psychoactive Substances (NPS) are a particular preoccupation of the UNODC. NPS is an umbrella term for psychoactive plants such as *salvia divinorum*, kratom and khat, and a range of chemicals that are not included in the UN classification of narcotics. Over 540 different types of NPS were reported in 2019, the 'tip of the iceberg' with over 2,000 different types of NPS estimated to be in circulation. This covers derivative substances distinguished from controlled drugs by minor molecular changes, and 'mimetics' that are chemically different from controlled drugs but claim to mimic the effects of use. These include cathinones (marketed as alternatives to cocaine or amphetamine) and synthetic cannabinoids (synthetic cannabis).

Markets for NPS have been largely concentrated in the industrial countries of North America, Europe and Australasia, and among the 15–24 age group, prisoners and homeless populations.

Cocaine

Despite the attention given to cocaine within international drug control, US foreign policy and Netflix docudramas, the drug has traditionally been the least consumed of the high-profile narcotics. The UNODC estimated 23 million users in 2023. Australia, Ireland, Spain, the US and the UK were the leading cocaine consumer countries. Persistent and cheap supply from Latin America is enabling cocaine to make inroads into a competitive market in which the position of synthetics has strengthened.

Increased accessibility of high purity cocaine has led to an increase in cocaine-related fatalities. In England, which recorded the twelfth consecutive annual rise in drug deaths in 2023, 1,188 fatalities involved cocaine. This was a 30 per cent increase from the previous year. In Scotland, 41 per cent of the record number of overdose deaths reported in 2023 were linked to cocaine and cocaine-injecting, compared to 6 per cent of fatalities in 2017.

Risky behaviours

Criminalization has not deterred the use of drugs. The UNODC data demonstrates that demand for illicit substances thrives decades into a global prohibition. The reasons for sustained demand, and the ineffectiveness of sanctions are explored in later chapters. Here, it's worth noting that as the use and types of substances available has increased, so have numbers of people engaging in risky drug use behaviours such as injecting and polydrug use.

It is estimated that there are 13.9 million people who inject drugs (PWID). The sharing of injecting equipment is a 'leading contributor' to illness, disease and death, according to a *Lancet* review. The 2023 UNODC *World Drug Report* estimates that 6.6 million people who inject drugs live with Hepatitis C (HCV), 1.6 million with HIV and 1.4 million with both HIV and HCV. PWID are commonly exposed to other risks and vulnerabilities. This includes homelessness, unstable housing, incarceration, sex work and intimate partner violence.

The largest populations of PWID are in Russia, China and the USA, while Georgia and the Seychelles have been among those with the highest prevalence of injecting drug use. Injecting is predominantly a male behaviour – one in five injecting users are women, but the demographics of PWID vary across regions; for example, injecting is concentrated among older, long-term users in Europe and North America. By contrast, South America, Eastern Europe and countries in the Middle East and North Africa (MENA) region have growing populations of young injectors.

Opioids are the most injected drugs. They are a leading cause of treatment demand and drug-related fatality but are being overtaken by injection-related harms that involve other water-soluble drugs such as cocaine, NPS, amphetamines and benzodiazepines, sometimes administered in combination with opioids, and fuelling drug-related deaths.

Also record highs: drug supply under criminalization

Given evidently wide public access to narcotics, it is inevitable that 'record seizures' belie a more complex supply-side picture. From this perspective, the drug hauls that are routinely paraded by law enforcement are simply a factor of increased supply and a larger market. They do not indicate progress in containing illicit drug volumes. Back to our data snapshot to illustrate this point.

In 2020, the global area under opium poppy cultivation was 'substantially larger' than a decade earlier, according to the UNODC. Afghanistan saturated the market, a hub for three-quarters of illicit global opium farming. Over 224,000 hectares (ha) were planted with opium poppy, enabling potential opium production of 6,300 metric tonnes and around 450 metric tonnes of heroin. Myanmar, Mexico and Laos contributed modest amounts to record international cultivation levels.

In relation to coca for cocaine manufacture, the UNODC reported a 'massive upward trend over the period 2013–17, during which the area under coca bush cultivation more than doubled'. In 2019, 234,200 ha were illicitly planted with coca, allowing the highest level ever of potential global cocaine manufacture at 1,784 metric tonnes. As with the concentration of opium poppy supply in Afghanistan, Colombia accounted for more than half of the world's illicit coca cultivation. And like Myanmar, Mexico and Laos in global opiate supply, Peru and Bolivia played the sweeper role in coca cultivation, contributing modestly at the margins of the main action, but always ready to take up the slack.

Over six decades since the UN 1961 UN Single Convention on Drugs proscribed the unauthorized cultivation of narcotic plants, unauthorized cannabis cultivation is also thriving and is widespread globally. Countries including Morocco, Afghanistan, India, Pakistan, Lebanon and Albania have traditionally been the main source of cannabis herb and resin. This picture is changing as new technologies such as home growing kits and specialized seed breeding make it possible for people to cultivate at home, and in countries with hostile temperatures and seasons. Half of all UN member states report increasing levels of indoor cultivation to UN drug control bodies.

Illegal synthetic manufacture is also at record volumes as manufacture zones proliferate. Methamphetamine supply has 'undergone remarkable changes in the last decade […] global seizure quantities growing more than 6 times since 2008'.

In the Americas, Mexico displaced the US as the hub of methamphetamine manufacture after the 2005 US Combat Methamphetamine Act limited access to over-the-counter medicines containing ephedrine and pseudoephedrine, the precursors used for methamphetamine home production. There had been 24,000 US Drug Enforcement Administration (DEA) methamphetamine-related seizures in the US in 2004 alone, the year before the new federal measure.

Central and West European countries are another source of international illicit methamphetamine supply, according to a 2022 report by the European Monitoring Centre for Drugs and Drug Addiction (EMCDDA). Afghanistan adds to a congested picture. An increase in ephedra plant cultivation in provinces such as Herat, Nimroz and Farah competitively positioned the country as a source of low-cost, plant-based methamphetamine.

According to the UNODC, Interpol, and US agencies such as the DEA, the Department of Justice and the Office of National Drug Control Policy (ONDCP), China and India are the weakest links in the chain of precursor chemical controls. The two countries have been highlighted as the primary export location of dual-use industrial chemicals used in drug manufacture, and of NPS drugs. Alongside Mexico, they are cited by experts as the principal manufacture zones for illicit fentanyl shipped to countries like Canada and the US (China), and tramadol to West and East Africa (India).

Hostile exchanges between the US and China on the fentanyl issue led China to suspend bilateral drug cooperation with the US in 2023, including drug-related extraditions. By contrast, Public Health Canada looked inward. A 2024 report conceded that laboratory interdictions in British Columbia, Ontario and Alberta 'suggest that domestic supply is more than sufficient to supply the domestic market'.

* * *

If international drug control has underperformed in terms of demand and supply reduction, how about that other crucial responsibility of ensuring access to essential medicines? Since my fateful 1997 conversation in the Garden of Reflection, there has been little improvement. The title of a 2023 World Health Organization (WHO) publication *Left Behind in Pain* tells you all you need to know about progress. A 2018 *Lancet* Commission described the lack of access to pain relief medication as 'one of the most heinous, hidden inequities in global health'.

How do we account for these poor results and why, despite an evidently urgent need for policy change, do we appear to be locked into a wholly counterproductive strategy? If that illicit cannabis smoker is still with us, let's explore the roots of your criminality.

2
BUILDING AN INTERNATIONAL DRUG PROHIBITION

If presented with a blank slate to devise a new, evidence-led approach to psychoactive substance management, we would likely not choose criminalization. Not if we consider the results detailed in the previous chapter and we are prepared to move beyond our own prejudices that decades of criminalization norms have instilled.

Most of the harms which we associate with drugs, and which are used to justify the criminalization approach, flow from criminalization strategies. For example, overdose deaths are a result of the policy choice not to regulate substance quality and purity. In a global consumer market of an estimated 300 million people, this makes for a lot of poisoned users.

Similarly, violence is a characteristic of a complex international trade that has flourished under criminalization, is valued at an estimated annual US$650 billion, but which has no formal mechanisms of negotiation or arbitration.

Policy in a silo: the exceptionalism of drug control

In many other aspects, criminalization strategy is counterproductive for achieving goals of reduced supply, access and harm. Drug policy processes, and the way in which strategy is determined and evaluated, are also unfit for modern purpose.

Drugs are a cross-cutting policy issue, intersecting with areas such as health, development and education. There are many stakeholders that we would want to bring into the design and assessment of a new, modern approach. This includes people with living or lived experience of illicit drug markets. How would we otherwise know if our new direction was doing good and achieving goals, or if we were off course and causing unintended harm?

In other areas of public policy, the neoliberal revolution of the 1980s transformed citizens who held public entitlements into clients of competitive education, healthcare and other public service provision. New Public Management agendas emphasized the importance of 'consumer' voice and choice. Schools, hospitals and other public services were required to be efficient, transparent and accountable to users. This is not and never has been the case in national and international drug policy processes, which criminalize and exclude the voice of service users and drug policy 'clients'. This contradicts Human Rights-Based Approaches (HRBA), which centre stakeholder participation in all aspects of design and implementation, as captured in the slogan 'Nothing about us without us'. For Amartya Sen, winner of the 1998 Nobel Prize in Economics, HRBA are essential to redress discriminatory practices and inequalities, and for the realization of fundamental rights.

As for the mainstreaming of rights-based and gender-sensitive approaches in policy and programmes, recall that in many countries, enforcement is associated with police violence, arbitrary detention and mandatory execution. Drug policy is not open or accountable and it certainly does not prioritize vulnerable groups in the policy measures that impact their lives. It is closed off, securitized and almost exclusively the responsibility of law enforcement actors. Interagency collaboration is weak, both within the UN system and in national criminal justice administration. Rather than engagement with cross-cutting areas to ensure strategies do not clash, drug policy exists in a silo, detached from human rights obligations and from best practice approaches.

Drug policy actors do not produce impact or outcome assessments of operations, other than as this relates to the metrics of the UN system. We may have giddy police reporting of record drug seizures, but law enforcement rarely assesses the impact of these same seizures on neighbourhood markets, distribution networks, local drug-related violence or the price and purity of substitute drugs that inevitably fill the vacated market share.

International law enforcement and 'counternarcotics' policing absorbs an annual US$100 billion. The sector is peculiarly immune to the rigours of financial evaluation and spending cuts that have scythed through most other forms of public spending.

A modern, revised drug policy would also move on from the one-size-fits-all approach of the current system. For example, the United Nations Office on Drugs and Crime (UNODC) acknowledges that most of the 300 million adults who use controlled drugs do so irregularly, moderately and without adverse health or other consequences. By contrast, an estimated sixty million people have a drug use disorder. This includes both those with a drug dependence, which is associated with substance tolerance and withdrawal symptoms, and those with a drug addiction, defined as drug use related behavioural changes. Drug prohibition and policing homogenize all users as criminal. Specific needs and vulnerabilities are not targeted.

The criminalization approach and drug policy processes are atypical in terms of lack of scrutiny and accountability, weak stakeholder engagement, and an apparent exemption from science and evidence.

As a starting point for a new approach, we might consider the potential of mind- and mood-altering substances to cause harm, both directly to the user and indirectly to others. Fortunately for our purposes, scientific experts have done this. In 2007, David Nutt, Professor of Neuropsychopharmacology and chair of the British government's Advisory Council on the Misuse of Drugs (ACMD), and colleagues published a groundbreaking article in *The Lancet*. This developed a nine-category matrix of harm based on three dimensions of evaluation: physical health effects on the user; potential for dependence; and harm to others (social harm). Alcohol came top of the chart, with Nutt stating: 'I believe that the challenge of dealing with the harms of alcohol is probably the biggest challenge that we have in relation to drug harms today.'

Alcohol was followed (in order) by heroin, cocaine, and the psychotropic benzodiazepines such as Diazepam (Valium), Alprazolam (Xanax) and Chlordiazepoxide (Librium). 'Benzos' are prescribed for nervous illness such as anxiety, insomnia and seizures. They are sometimes used in combination with heroin to enhance sedative effects. Benzos are also available as a 'street drug' – illicit synthetic copies of the pharmaceutical medicine. Underscoring the harm of these unauthorized medications, benzodiazepines are a factor in over 70 per cent of drug-related deaths in Scotland.

Box 2.1: Scotland's drug-related deaths

Scotland's drug-related fatalities are a scandal. Its death rate of 277 per million is second only to the US. By way of comparison with other developed countries, the figure for the Netherlands is 17 drug-related fatalities per million, in Portugal it is 10 per million and in Japan it is two. Even Russia, which launched a ferocious crackdown on drug users and services, appears below Scotland, at a reported 68 deaths per million.

Ecstasy was at the bottom end of *The Lancet* table. Professor Nutt was sacked from the ACMD in 2009 when he elaborated that, statistically, riding a horse is more dangerous than taking MDMA.

A rerun of the analysis in 2010 for the UK Independent Scientific Committee on Drugs expanded the number of psychoactive substances to 20, adding seven additional evaluation criteria. Alcohol stayed at the top, with heroin, methamphetamine, cocaine and tobacco following. Ecstasy remained at the least harmful end alongside the hallucinogenic LSD.

These findings, and a weight of other scientific evidence, do not align with the classification of drug harms set out in the UN drug treaties, which, as we saw in Chapter 1, guides the severity of criminal sentencing for drug-related offences. We'll return to the classification system later. Here, it is worth emphasizing LSD and MDMA are Schedule I drugs under the 1971 Convention on Psychotropic Substances, determined to have a high abuse potential and no therapeutic value. As with the plant-based Schedule I substances cocaine, coca leaf, cannabis and heroin in the 1961 UN Single Convention, unauthorized transactions involving these least harmful synthetics attract the severest penalties.

There are many questions to ask of prohibition goals and criminalization strategy: where did this approach come from, and why have better results not been achieved given the extraordinary international consensus between all countries on criminalization and the immense financial resources dedicated to enforcing an underperforming model?

Box 2.2: Drug scheduling in the UK

In the UK, drug scheduling and criminal penalties for drug-related offences are set out in an over 50-year-old drug law, the 1971 Misuse of Drugs Act. The maximum penalty for possession of Class A (Schedule I) substances is seven years in prison, an unlimited fine or both. The penalty for manufacture and supply of LSD and MDMA, as well as of other Class A substances such as crack cocaine and methamphetamine, is life in prison, an unlimited fine or both.

Class B drugs include cannabis, amphetamine, synthetic cannabinoids and ketamine. Possession of these drugs carries the possibility of a maximum five years in prison, unlimited fine, or both. As with the Class A drugs, the penalty for supply-related offences is severe, with a maximum 14-year prison sentence. (Cannabis was a Class C substance from 2004 to 2009.)

Possession of Class C substances, including the plant khat (farmed in East Africa), piperazines (used to cut Ecstasy tablets) and the depressant GHB (Gamma-Hydroxybutyrate, notorious as a 'date rape' drug), carries a maximum two-year sentence, unlimited fine, or both, with supply offences facing a maximum 14 years, the same as for supplying Class B drugs.

The 2016 Psychoactive Substances Act sets out a maximum seven-year sentence for involvement in the supply or production of NPS, an unlimited fine, or both.

A historical trawl through the evolution of the UN treaty system explains criminalization failings *and* why criminalization policy cannot be revised or adjusted, despite failure to achieve the prohibition goals.

Constructing anti-drug norms: myth, women and race in the US prohibition movement

In Chapter 1, we saw that the late nineteenth and early twentieth century was a period of advocacy for regulation of consumer goods and for controls on intoxication. Campaigns to prevent the availability and misuse of alcohol in the UK, the US and colonial territories such as Australia and India were influential. They were also interconnected, cohering under an umbrella of Protestant churches, missionaries, philanthropists, anti-imperialists, social reformers and women's suffrage and anti-slavery campaigners. As detailed by Mark Schrad, 'nearly every major Black abolitionist and civil rights leader before World War I – from Frederick Douglass, Martin Delany and Sojourner Truth to F.E.W. Harper, Ida B. Wells, W.E.B. Du Bois, and Booker T. Washington – endorsed temperance and prohibition'.

While unified on the harms caused by the unregulated use of distilled spirits such as gin and whisky and other alcoholic beverages, national campaigns came from different ideological and religious perspectives. In the UK, a moderate stream promoting temperance dominated. This acknowledged the possibility of individuals exercising self-restraint in their drinking behaviours. The perspective was represented by organizations such as the Quakers, and prominent philanthropist and York-based chocolatier Joseph Rowntree. The temperance position problematized alcohol misuse as a contributing factor to poverty and called for social reforms to address the vulnerabilities of the poor to ill health and intemperate drinking habits, such as inadequate housing.

In the US, by contrast, the anti-alcohol campaign was evangelical and absolutist. The danger of alcohol was deemed severe, a single drop causing physical and spiritual impoverishment. This movement lobbied state and federal government for a complete ban on alcohol.

The US alcohol prohibition movement is important for explaining the emergence and the intellectual direction of drug policy, and the roots of the drug laws that we have today – over a century later. Organizations influential in the US prohibition campaign included the Prohibition Party, the Woman's Christian Temperance Union, and the Anti-Saloon League, all founded in Ohio, in 1869, 1874 and 1893 respectively. Leaning into the movement's evangelical base, these groups claimed that alcohol was a means of demonic possession. As discussed by Richard DeGrandpre in his highly recommended *The Cult of Pharmacology* (2006), psychoactive substances were ascribed 'a unique spirit or essence', making them able to 'bypass all social conditioning of the mind' and 'enter into the body and take possession of it'. Images and narratives of individual enslavement to alcohol were prominent in prohibition propaganda. Abstinence and prayer were promoted as the key to salvation and freedom.

To galvanize the God-fearing, Christian American community, prohibition campaigners emphasized the link between intoxication and 'outsiders'. This populist tack played to the dislocation and suspicions generated by mass immigration. Nearly 25 million people, predominantly young males from Ireland, Italy, Poland and Germany, arrived in the country between 1865 and 1915. The influx of beer-, wine- and spirit-drinking foreigners added to an existing problem of heavy liquor consumption in the US. Prohibition campaigners argued that the saloon bars, gambling dens and brothels that catered to this large cohort of men were hubs of vice, and a threat to decency. Sites of impropriety were a focus of direct action and activist meetings to 'pray away' the dangers posed to Christian American women and children.

Prohibition narratives drew heavily on early social Darwinist and eugenicist ideas that were increasingly influential in the second half of the nineteenth century. This included the work of British polymath Herbert Spencer, whose 1864 publication *Principles of Biology* applied Charles Darwin's theory of evolution and natural selection to human society. The interpretation of 'survival of the fittest' as a competition between different ethnic races was developed in the writing of eugenicists such as Darwin's cousin Francis Galton, who argued that intelligence was hereditary. Selective breeding of the highest-evolved race, designated as the white race, was proposed as a mechanism for improving the human stock and reducing numbers of other, less-evolved populations that were a drain on finite resources of land and food. In his 1869 publication *Hereditary Genius*, Galton outlined that, just as dogs and horses can be bred to have 'peculiar powers […] so it would be quite practicable to produce a highly-gifted race of men by judicious marriages during several consecutive generations'.

Eugenicists fretted over the potential causes of white decline. Galton believed there existed 'social agencies […] working towards the degradation of human nature'. Alcoholism and miscegenation (racial 'interbreeding') were two of the greatest threats. These were heavily conflated in the propaganda of the US alcohol prohibition lobby. For example, in a December 1914 congressional speech on the urgency of a federal alcohol ban, Richmond P. Hobson, representative for Alabama and key figure in the Anti-Saloon League, set out that 'All life in the universe is founded upon the principle of evolution. Alcohol directly reverses that principle.' From there, he claimed different racial impacts of drinking:

> Liquor promptly degenerates the red man, throws him back into savagery […] Liquor will actually make a brute out of a negro, causing him to commit unnatural crimes. The effect is the same on the white man, though the white man being further evolved it takes longer time to reduce him to the same level. Starting young, however, it does not take a very long time to speedily cause a man in the forefront of civilization to pass through the successive stages and

become semi civilized, semi savage, savage, and, at last, below the brute.

After achieving alcohol prohibition (albeit temporarily) with the Eighteenth Amendment to the US Constitution, which was ratified in 1919, the gaze of the prohibition lobby fell on other devilish, narcotic substances. Hobson himself went on to establish the International Narcotic Education Association in 1923.

The association between 'outsiders', demonic substances and white racial decline was highly effective in the campaign for alcohol prohibition. The use of *metonymy*, defined as 'the act of referring to something using a word that describes one of its qualities or features', infused the wider campaign for a sober, pure and godlier nation. This was to be achieved by also banning opiates, cocaine and marijuana (cannabis), all legal, commonly consumed and globally traded commodities at the turn of the twentieth century. It was an outlandish idea at the time. In the early 1900s demand for these plants and derivative products was booming in the US and globally.

The 'trade in poison'

Starting with the identification of morphine in the opium poppy in 1807, advances in chemistry allowed for the isolation of analgesic and stimulant alkaloids in plant materials. The discovery of morphine was followed in 1859 by the identification of cocaine in the coca leaf. Demand for the plants soared. There was a surge in commercial and pharmaceutical investment in the manufacture of morphine and cocaine-based medicines, tonics, supplements and 'pick-me-ups'.

These products were popular in Western Europe, North America and in settler colonies, where they could be purchased from grocers' stores and mail order catalogues. They were administered for a range of diseases, pains and complaints in adults and in children, from cocaine toothache drops for toddlers to injecting morphine solution for neurasthenia ('women's problems').

Coca

Peru's coca economy developed in the second half of the nineteenth century through two commercial chains. The Germanic-Andean circuit saw European pharmaceutical investment in coca leaf farming and cocaine manufacture in Peru for export to Germany and Austria. This peaked in 1901 at around 10,700 kilos, as cocaine revolutionized anaesthesia, replacing the notorious killer chloroform in surgical procedures.

In the US-Andean circuit, Peruvian coca leaf was exported to the US for cocaine manufacture by firms such as Parke-Davies Company and Burroughs Wellcome for wellbeing and endurance potions Vin Mariani, Forced March and Coca-Cola. Developed by Atlanta pharmacist Dr John Pemberton and introduced in 1886, Coca-Cola was marketed as a cure for headaches, fatigue and nausea. The manufacturer was forced to revise the drink's secret recipe in the 1920s due to the alcohol content.

Between 1877 and 1905, Peruvian coca leaf exports increased from 7 metric tonnes to a staggering 850 metric tonnes. Peru's principal commercial rival was Java (Indonesia), where the Dutch colonists transplanted coca cultivation for cocaine manufacture. Between 1904 and 1910, Java coca leaf exports increased from 23 metric tonnes to 400 metric tonnes.

The opium economy and opium wars

According to the historian Alfred McCoy, 'opium was fully integrated into the commerce and consumer cultures of Asia and the West'. Poppies were farmed in a giant arc running from the Balkans through Persia to British-administered India. A vast opium sector employed farmers, packers, transporters, brokers, shippers, porters and clerks. Cultivation for export was historically concentrated in British India. Over 1.5 million households in Bengal and Malwa farmed poppy under British permits and pressure.

In the first half of the nineteenth century, the US and European market for manufactured opium and derivative (morphine) products was less significant than the market for smoking opium in colonial territories. Colonial licensing systems and taxes on opium farmers, retailers and smokers generated around half of administrative income in British-controlled Singapore and a third of revenues in Hong Kong. In French Indochina (Vietnam and Cambodia), the Spanish-controlled Philippines and the Dutch East Indies (Indonesia), a similar model of monopoly opium sales to local smokers contributed 10 to 20 per cent of income.

China was a key target for British opium merchants, who sought to prise open the 'closed empire' of the Qing dynasty (1644–1912) and access to Chinese silks, porcelain and precious stones. Opium smoking spread rapidly in China as British traders (and local consumers) defied bans imposed by the Daoguang Emperor and smuggled chests of opium into Canton (Guangzhou). The Qing dynasty fought and lost two opium wars (1839–42 and 1856–60) against British merchants backed by the Royal Navy in their aggressive campaign of commercial penetration of China.

Defeat during the ensuing 'Century of Humiliation' required China to accept Indian opium imports and facilitate the trade by surrendering ports such as Hong Kong to the British. As *The Economist* outlined in a 2017 article, 'Every Chinese schoolchild knows that the modern drive for wealth and power is, at root, a means of avenging the Opium Wars and what followed.'

The authority of the Qing dynasty was drastically eroded by the opium wars. Having been forced to accept opium imports, Chinese authorities could not suppress the re-emergence and growth of domestic opium poppy cultivation in China. By 1906, China was itself the source of 85 per cent of the 38,000 metric tonnes of opium on the international market.

In an interesting role reversal, the British government was by this time negotiating a bilateral agreement with China to reduce Indian opium exports to zero within a decade. Under the 1907 Sino-British Ten Years

Agreement, China correspondingly agreed to prevent domestic cultivation and use of opium.

Internal dissent, such as the Taiping Rebellion (1850–64) and Boxer Rebellion (1899–1901), and further military setbacks for China, including the First Sino-Japanese War of 1894–95, accelerated the collapse of the Qing dynasty in 1912. Chinese migrants fleeing economic crisis and the chaos of imperial disintegration re-established cultures of opium smoking in host countries. Smoking dens for the Chinese diaspora were common in port cities such as Liverpool, San Francisco and Amsterdam, and in British and Dutch colonial territories of the Far East such as Malaysia, Indonesia and Singapore.

The US offered opportunities on the West Coast and employment in mining, railroad construction and agriculture. In 1860 there were an estimated 35,000 Chinese in a US population of 31.5 million. By 1880, numbers had increased to an estimated 105,000 people. They faced intense hostility from European migrants, anti-Chinese agitation by US labour unions, and institutionalized discrimination. The 1882 Chinese Exclusion Act halted immigration from China and prevented Chinese migrants from becoming naturalized US citizens. Historic state-level anti-miscegenation laws that forbade inter-racial relationships was extended to the Chinese. For example, the Civil Code in California was amended in 1880 to restrict marriage between whites and 'Mongolians'.

The White Man's burden: US prohibition leadership on the international stage

The use of metonymy and racialization of substance use imagery to fire the US alcohol prohibition campaign also shaped agitation against other ethnic and racial groups and against other ungodly substances, such as opium and cocaine, and cannabis, which grew wild across the US.

This interlinkage initially focused on Chinese migrants (opium), extending to 'cocainized' African Americans, and Mexican smokers of another devilish, and allegedly foreign, substance, *Maria Juana*. Newspapers, radio and town hall events provided a platform for prohibition campaigners to terrify their audiences with tales of insanity and murder linked to the use of these everyday medicines and groceries. Prohibition propaganda focused on the particular vulnerability of white women and youth to non-white male outsiders purveying intoxication. Dime novels, pulp fiction magazines, and cinema films developed and normalized lurid caricatures such as the 'yellow peril' of villainous opium-smoking Chinese. The criminal mastermind Fu Manchu, created by the British writer Sax Rohmer in 1913, popularized the notion of a devilish Chinese cunning and evil.

Alongside the 'yellow peril', the US was also home to 'yellow journalism' and the New York media empires of Joseph Pulitzer and William Randolph Hearst. Both proprietors pushed sensationalist reporting on corruption, crime and murder in circulation wars of the 1890s. These commonly featured exaggerated claims from the prohibition lobby among other stories involving foreigners, deviance, intoxication and violence.

A notorious 1914 *New York Times* article by Edward Huntington Williams MD, 'Negro Cocaine "Fiends" Are A New Southern Menace', claimed 'murder and insanity' were increasing among 'lower class blacks' with a habit of 'cocainism' and resulting in 'homicidal attacks upon innocent and unsuspecting victims'.

Racism and xenophobia in prohibition propaganda served many uses. For Michelle Alexander, it was intended to dehumanize non-white communities, portraying them as less deserving of rights. Subsequent state and federal anti-drug initiatives served as 'new Jim Crow laws', obstructing Black citizenship and maintaining racial segregation and inequality long after human slavery had been abolished with the Thirteenth Amendment of the US Constitution ratified in 1865.

Prohibition agitation in the US parlayed into discriminatory and repressive federal anti-drug laws. This included the Opium Exclusion Act of 1909, which shut down opium dens, and the 1914 Harrison Narcotics Act, the first major US federal drug law. This imposed bureaucratic registration processes and taxes on those involved in importing, manufacturing, selling or distributing opiates and coca leaf. Over 5,000 physicians were jailed between 1915 and 1938 for unauthorized prescriptions and sales.

The 1937 Marihuana Tax Act, signed into law by President Franklin D. Roosevelt, incorporated cannabis into the taxation regime similarly with the intention of sharply reducing availability and use. US public opinion of a plant common in domestic agriculture (hemp) was swayed by the social media hysteria of the day: the 1936 film *Reefer Madness*.

International alliance-building for global action

US prohibition groups and Protestant missionaries overseas were not alone in their concern with the international opium trade and rates of opium use. Karl Marx was an early critic of the 'free trade in poison' at the heart of the British empire. In 1858, he wrote that British imperialism in India:

> forces the opium cultivation upon Bengal, to the great damage of the productive resources of that country; compels one part of the Indian *ryots* [peasants] to engage in the poppy culture; entices another part into the same by dint of money advances; [and] keeps the wholesale manufacture of the deleterious drug a close monopoly in its hands.

Four decades and little progress later, Quaker Member of the British Parliament (MP) Joseph Pease decried opium as 'universally the source of human misery, de-moralization, and crime', and Britain as 'a trader in the most obnoxious article you could imagine'. An 1891 Parliamentary resolution that he sponsored condemning the opium trade failed to gain support.

The anti-opium movement looked to transnational alliance-building and US leadership to advance an international agreement on controls. The transnational dimension of the campaign was influenced by the success of the alcohol prohibition movement, which pressured governments to collectively address issues that transcended national borders.

As European powers were scrambling to carve up the continent of Africa at the 1884–85 Berlin Conference, the anti-alcohol lobby argued European countries had to commit to promoting the health and moral well-being of 'native' populations. There was notable success at the 1889 Brussels Anti-Slavery Conference. Alongside agreement to combat Arab enslavement of Black Africans, the final 1890 Brussels Conference Act acknowledged European responsibility for improving the spiritual and moral condition of native populations. This included through restrictions on European alcohol exports to Africa and on the manufacture of local alcoholic brews in Africa, and a ban on alcohol drinking by non-white populations.

Reformers welcomed the Brussels Act and racial segregation in alcohol markets as concern for the wellbeing of Black Africans. A scan of conference statements and media coverage reveals more of the shockingly racist language and eugenicist narratives that seeped through US domestic campaigns against outsiders. Blacks were infantilized and portrayed as less evolved than white colonial rulers, or as gun-toting drunken 'savages' that posed a mortal threat to colonial bureaucrats and white settlers. By way of an example, a quote from the London *Pall Mall Gazette* in support of the Brussels Act:

> We have heard the African native spoken of often as a child. We ought to realize that to allow firearms and gin to pass freely into Africa is literally as mischievous as to allow them to circulate in a nursery.

Transnational mobilization was a highly effective strategy, leading to agreement between states to restrict the export of both alcohol and guns.

Anti-opium campaigners similarly looked to international-level agreement between states to stop colonial exploitation and halt the flow of opium. It was a position that was supported by the US government. In 1898, the US acquired the Philippines following defeat of Spain in the 1898 Spanish–American war (in which Richmond P. Hobson incidentally came to prominence as a naval hero), and thereby the Spanish monopoly on opium sales in the territory. US Republican presidents William McKinley (1897–1901) and Theodore Roosevelt (1901–09) stepped into the vacuum of international leadership on the opium issue, promising a 'civilizing mission' that would free populations from European misrule, opium slavery, and obstacles to Christian conversion.

As immortalized in Rudyard Kipling's 1899 poem, Presidents McKinley and Roosevelt assumed 'The White Man's Burden' towards their 'new-caught sullen peoples,|Half devil and half child' and convened the first international opium conference. This was held in Shanghai, China, in 1909, and was simultaneously a US initiative to rebuild diplomatic relations with the Chinese emperor.

Over the following century, the US morphed from fractious former British colony to global superpower. 'Drugs' play an important role in this story. In the terminology of William McAllister, a succession of US presidents leveraged 'narcodiplomacy' and bilateral country cooperation on plant controls to build geostrategic alliances, advance commercial opportunities and influence the policing and security architecture of foreign countries.

By the 2000s, US agencies overseas working on drug-related policy included 80 Drug Enforcement Administration offices in 58 countries, 50 Office of Investigations of the Department of Homeland Security international offices, and the Narcotics Affairs Sections of US embassies worldwide.

Crafting an international structure of narcotic regulation

In the early 1900s, global powers were at a critical juncture and forced to consider issues of addiction, exploitation and demands for controls on opium cultivation, exports and smoking.

Global conferences were much smaller events in those days; vast swathes of the world were represented by imperial powers. Britain, Austria-Hungary, France, Germany, Italy, Japan, the Netherlands, Persia, Portugal, Russia and Siam (Thailand) sent representatives to the 1909 Shanghai meeting convened by the US and China. It was a landmark event, establishing the principle that national governments and colonial authorities should work collaboratively to protect citizens and subjects from the exploitation of the opium trade. Having reached agreement at the conference that opiates were harmful, and use should be limited to medical purposes, not languid recreation and wellbeing tonics, the US federal government and evangelicals lobbied for binding commitments on cultivation and consumption bans, or what the UNODC refers to in its 2009 *World Drug Report* as 'an unambiguous prohibitionist global drug regime'.

Such a move was unthinkable for the more liberal and secular Europeans, who saw a ban as unenforceable and unnecessary. France, Germany, Italy, the Netherlands, Portugal and the UK did sign up to the subsequent 1912 Hague International Opium Convention. As outlined by former UNODC Director General Yury Fedotov at a 2012 centenary event, the Hague Treaty 'formally established narcotics' control as a fundamental element of international law [and] established the groundwork for the evolving international system of drug control'.

The 1912 Convention (in Chapter 2, Article 6) set out measures for the 'gradual and effective suppression' of opium and restrictions on cocaine and heroin exports, a major triumph for the prohibition lobby, but to accommodate the Europeans, there was no specific timeframe.

At the end of the First World War in 1918, the number of state parties to the 1912 Treaty increased to nearly sixty, as signatories of the Versailles Peace Treaties automatically became parties to the Convention, administered and overseen by the new League of

Nations. From then on, regime-building through to the present day has been a process of layering new treaties and agreements onto founding principles.

In the inter-war period, five League of Nations drug conventions were negotiated: these restricted consumption of opiate and cocaine products; required licensing and monitoring of stocks, imports and exports; and imposed annual reporting requirements on states. A two-tier schedule of narcotic drug harm was agreed to guide states in the sanctions regime that they were required to impose for unauthorized transactions. This classificatory system incorporated other substances deemed harmful and as recommended by the Health Committee of the League of Nations (forerunner of the World Health Organization). Cannabis was brought into the regulatory framework in 1925.

Direction and administration for the new international system was provided by an eight-country Opium Advisory Committee (OAC) to the League of Nations, established in 1921. This was supported by the Permanent Central Opium Board (PCOB), created by the 1925 Geneva Convention with a mandate (Article 24) to 'watch the course of the international trade', monitor for excess accumulation of stocks, prevent countries 'becoming a center for the illicit traffic' and calculate permissible levels of cultivation, manufacture, imports and exports.

The inter-war regulatory system managed to make serious inroads in reducing the size of the opiate and cocaine sectors. By 1934, global opium production had fallen 60 per cent from 1906/07. Heroin manufacture decreased from 20,000 pounds to 2,200 pounds between 1926 and 1931. The earlier 1907 Sino-British agreement had removed the bulk of opium from global markets.

Coca leaf exports from Java and Peru plummeted by nearly 90 per cent. Until resuscitation by a new class of coca exporters in the 1970s, the Peruvian coca sector went into collapse.

Progress was undermined by national concerns over state sovereignty and security in the building tensions that led to the Second World War. Some countries were unwilling to be bound by the League's restrictions on opium imports (Japan and Germany) and cultivation (Iran and Turkey). Political and military leaders wanted autonomy in the procurement and development of medicines for conflict conditions and improving endurance and treatment of injury. Japanese-owned heroin-, morphine- and cocaine-manufacturing facilities sprang up across occupied China in the early 1930s, and Java and Turkey became the primary sources of both pharmaceutical and unauthorized opium.

Wartime conditions of surveillance and global conflict limited the diversion and trafficking of substances regulated by the League of Nations treaties. In the immediate post-war period of the late 1940s, the drug situation was not a pressing concern for countries levelled by war. It was, however, for the US, which moved quickly to resuscitate the issue on the international stage, and in conditions that were highly favourable for advancing a narcotic prohibition agenda.

The US, the UN and the post-war criminalization regime

Historians of international drug policy see a sharp divide between the inter-war (1919–39) League of Nations treaties regulating the trade in opiates, cocaine and derivatives, and the post-war period of UN drug control (recommended readings are listed at the end of this book). Neil Boister's assessment of the post-war direction as a 'suppression regime' is helpful in explaining a seismic shift.

In the post-war period, starting with the 1961 United Nations Single Convention, international policy and national reporting mechanisms are far less concerned with regulating legitimate access to essential medicines. The international framework that was constructed after the war and crafted by the US is instead dedicated to proactively and coercively eliminating unauthorized markets. In sum, imposing the long-held US goal of an international prohibition.

Post-war occupation of the defeated Axis countries positioned US forces to destroy manufacturing facilities, requisition new synthetic innovations such as Amidon (methadone) and Pethidin (pethidine) developed by the Nazi regime and influence strict, new national drug laws in countries under US administration. This included Japan and targeting an epidemic of methamphetamine misuse. This stimulant drug had been available without restrictions under the brand name Philopon since 1941. After the surrender of Japan, a flood of these 'wake-amines' intended for the Japanese airforce were diverted to black markets. The 1951 Stimulant Drug Control Law and the 1953 Narcotics Control Law empowered (US-trained) law enforcement to aggressively repress methamphetamine and opiate markets. Foregrounding the imbalance was to develop in the international 'suppression regime', an amended 1954 Opium Law was required to encourage farmers to cultivate opium poppy in response to a chronic shortage of medicines.

Other post-war factors favourable to the US advancing a drug criminalization agenda included the dependence of European countries on US financial support for post war reconstruction. This weakened the liberal wall of diplomatic resistance to the US prohibition vision that had prevailed during the inter-war period.

The US did not have to employ pressure on all states to force them into alignment with the prohibitive ethos of the 1961 UN Single Convention. Criminalization strategies and punishment regimes outlined in the 1961 treaty had utility for governments across the world that were facing the instability of decolonization, counter-cultural rebellion, anti-war protests and civil rights agitation. In a famous quote cited by Dan Baum in a 2016 *Harper's Magazine* article, John Ehrlichman, Richard Nixon's policy adviser, explained:

> We knew we couldn't make it illegal to be either against the war or black, but by getting the public to associate the hippies with marijuana and blacks with heroin, and then criminalizing both heavily, we could disrupt those communities [...] arrest their leaders, raid their homes,

break up their meetings, and vilify them night after night on the evening news.

Selective and targeted enforcement easily translated to other national contexts. Drug criminalization was a useful tool for governments to discredit and demobilize critics and opponents, and to lay the norms and expectations of post-war societies.

The abject disinterest of the Soviet Union in the narcotics issue gave the US carte blanche in crafting the new international framework. For Soviet leaders, substance misuse was a problem specific to Western capitalist societies, bred in an environment of exploitation and alienation. As these conditions allegedly did not exist in the Soviet Union or among its satellite states in Central and Eastern Europe, Moscow had nothing to report or contribute. Like many of the assumptions of the Soviet leadership, this proved to be catastrophic error.

As at the turn of the twentieth century, and in the founding meetings of drug control, developments in China helped the US to push a hard-line prohibition agenda. The Chinese Communist Party undertook a ferocious anti-opium drive after taking power in 1949. The 1950 'Circular on Strict Prohibition of Opium and Drug Taking' and 1952 'Directive on Eradication of Drug Epidemic' introduced the forced eradication of opium poppies and compulsory detoxification programmes. The measures decimated historical opium poppy cultivation sites. An estimated twenty million people were entered into treatment programmes, and in 1952, the People's Republic was declared a 'drug-free nation'.

Change and continuity in the global governance of drugs

The US steered international approval of the key treaties of the post-war suppression regime, framed by the 1961 UN Single Convention (focused on plant-based substances), the follow-up 1971 UN Convention on Psychotropic Substances (synthetics) and the 1988 UN Convention against Illicit Traffic in Narcotic Drugs and Psychotropic Substances (precursor chemicals).

Although the post-war criminalization treaties mark a break from the regulatory approach of the early 1920s and 1930s, there is continuity with many founding ideas and organizations. The guiding principle that states must collaborate to combat illicit drugs – because the drug challenge transcends national borders – remained central to the post-war architecture. The role of international oversight and monitoring bodies was also retained in the move from the League of Nations to the United Nations.

With the post-war creation of the United Nations, treaty monitoring and oversight passed from the Opium Advisory Committee to a new policy executive, the current 53-country Commission on Narcotic Drugs (CND), with secretariat functions provided by the UNODC in Vienna.

The responsibilities of the inter-war Permanent Central Opium Board were assumed by a 13-member

International Narcotics Control Board (INCB), a treaty body created by the 1961 Convention to 'facilitate effective national action to attain the aims of this Convention' (Article 9, Clause 5). The INCB administers the estimate system for national medical and scientific requirements, and monitors country compliance through the statistical returns system. The system of classifying substances according to purported harm was also carried over from the pre-war regulatory model, as were the reporting metrics used to evaluate changes to agricultural commodity flows now used to police private human behaviours.

The next section provides a summary of the most important UN drug treaties. These create obligations in international law for signatory states, and they frame all our national drug laws.

The 1961 UN Single Convention on Narcotic Drugs

The inter-war schedule of controls for plant-based substances is extended from two classes to four.

Schedule I and (confusingly) Schedule IV are the most restrictive, reserved for 'narcotics' with no legitimate medical or scientific value, and high abuse potential. Schedule IV substances have 'particularly dangerous properties' and include heroin, and until 2021, cannabis.

Schedules II and III are reserved for preparations determined by the WHO Expert Committee on Dangerous Drugs to have less abuse potential and some clinical purpose, for example, the morphine derivative codeine.

In relation to cultivation of the plant raw materials, Article 49 sets out a 25-year schedule for the termination of all unauthorized cannabis and coca leaf cultivation (by 1989), telescoped to 15 years for opium poppy (by 1979). Unauthorized cultivation is criminalized.

Articles 23 and 24 allow for national opium and coca monopolies in traditional cultivating countries such as Bolivia, Peru, India, Turkey and Iran to smooth the transition from free markets to limited UN medical supply quotas (essential medicines) and for cultural use.

The punishment-as-deterrence ethos of the 1961 treaty runs deep. Article 36 requires national laws that consider drug-related offences of possession, supply, cultivation, manufacture and transportation 'serious' and 'liable to adequate punishment particularly by imprisonment or other penalties of deprivation of liberty'. Article 39 suggests circumstances in which national governments might introduce more severe punishment if 'necessary or desirable for the protection of the public health or welfare'.

The 1971 UN Convention on Psychotropic Substances

This treaty was an afterthought, synthetics having remained under the radar during deliberation of the 1961 Single Convention.

The Convention replicates the four-tier schedule of harm and associated sanctions. Schedule I drugs have no therapeutic value and pose a threat to public health.

They include LSD, MDMA and, as was subsequently to prove a headache for reformers, THC, the psychoactive component in cannabis, which is separately controlled under the 1961 Convention. Drugs that present a risk of abuse but moderate therapeutic value fall into Schedule II or III, including amphetamines and barbiturates.

The treaty bypasses the confusion of Schedule IV status in the 1961 Convention and follows a logical numerical ranking: Schedule IV drugs pose a minor public health risk and have high therapeutic value (tranquillizers such as diazepam).

The 1971 treaty is far less comprehensive than the 1961 Convention: many salts used in synthetic chemistry are omitted from the 1971 schedule, and scheduling does not align with scientific evidence on therapeutic use, as evidenced by Professor David Nutt and team in *The Lancet* article of 2007 discussed at the beginning of this chapter.

1988 UN Convention against Illicit Traffic in Narcotic Drugs and Psychotropic Substances

The final UN drug convention to date deepens international cooperation against drug trafficking, including preventing money laundering and organized crime, and the implementation of extradition agreements.

It treats possession as a serious criminal offence (Article 3) (accounting for the increase in prosecuted and incarcerated women), and it encourages tougher measures such as forfeiture and confiscation of assets linked to drug-related offences.

The treaty establishes a two-tier table of controls for precursor chemicals and reagents used in drug manufacture, such as safrole, piperonal and potassium permanganate (used in cocaine extraction).

* * *

Regardless of national regime type, level of development, religion or other variable that might influence deviation from a global norm, nation states have acceded to a common approach of criminalization and law enforcement-led strategies. These focus on coercive disruption of the illicit trade, and exemplary punishment of drug law offenders.

Over the decades, anti-drug collaboration between states has been reinforced as the drug threat has evolved, from the unregulated opium trade in the 1900s, to post-war anxiety over deviance and crime, and on to a post-Cold War (1989) concern with drug revenues financing new transnational security threats such as terrorism and organized crime.

As a model of consensus between states, global regime-building, and the internationalization of norms, drug control is a major feat of political, diplomatic, and social engineering. As a global policy to protect the 'health and welfare of mankind', prevent access to dangerous drugs, and ensure global access to essential pain-relieving medicines, it has been one of the most significant international and national policy failures of modern times.

3
THE PERSISTENCE OF THE DRUG USER

As the United Nations Office on Drugs and Crime (UNODC) acknowledged in 2009, drug control efforts have 'rarely proceeded according to plan [...] Traffickers have proven to be resilient and innovative opponents and cultivators difficult to deter. The number, nature, and sources of controlled substances have changed dramatically over the years. None of this could have been predicted at the outset.'

This chapter and the next explore *why* the institutions of international and national drug control and the strategy of drug criminalization fail to achieve ambitions of a world free from the danger of narcotic drugs. This chapter explores consumer aspects such as changes in drug use cultures, and the endurance of drug demand. Chapter 4 looks at supply-side issues and why six decades of criminalizing plants and psychoactive drug manufacture has failed to curb, let alone eliminate, volumes of drug supply.

Before that, and to frame subsequent discussion, let's return to the argument that international drug control is characterized by continuity, and the locking-in of founding approaches and ideas. This is despite a weight of evidence that many founding assumptions were fundamentally wrong.

Markets, states and behaviours: myth and reality under criminalization

As set out by the godfather of neoliberalism, Milton Friedman, 'Making prohibition work is like making water run uphill; it's against nature.'

The US prohibition lobby, as architects of postwar drug control, believed that fierce suppression of narcotic drug supply would drive up the price of drugs, pushing 'junkies' out of the market. With nobody to sell to, illicit entrepreneurs would be forced into other, legal, activities. Exactly the opposite has happened over the 60+ years of criminalization. Shortages of drugs created by seizures do indeed drive prices higher, particularly at the retail level. But this is only ever temporary and people are not pushed out of the illicit market. For several reasons. People with addiction and dependence will secure the monies to purchase regular drugs that have become more expensive because of police enforcement. As discussed earlier in relation to the ballooning prison population, theft, sex work and debt are common ways of finding the necessary extra cash. In the language of economists, demand is inelastic.

New drug supply also quickly fills the market share that is vacated by law enforcement interdictions. Competition for this space can be intense. This is because criminalization makes drug-related activities profitable, in particular when prices are higher after a seizure. Innovation in distribution networks is also incentivized as new suppliers seek to circumvent the successful law enforcement intervention that created the shortage in the first place.

As conceded in the 1988 UN Convention Against Illicit Traffic in Narcotic Drugs and Psychotropic Substances, 'illicit traffic generates large financial profits and wealth'. Prohibition transforms cheap – if not worthless – plants, shrubs and chemicals into an illicit trade with a total retail value higher than the GDP of 163 out of 184 countries in the world. The enforcement of criminalization is consequently associated with the displacement of illicit drug market activity into a different neighbourhood, country or geographic hub. This process is also referred to as 'ballooning' – squeezing at one end simply shifts the air to another part of the balloon.

The story of illicit drug markets since the 1961 UN Single Convention and national criminalization laws is one of constant splintering, scattering and fragmentation incentivized by the added value created by criminalization. Seizures, eradications and arrests catalyze the relocation and reconfiguration of drug supply networks and organizations, changes in the types of drugs that are available, drug price and drug purity.

In relation to trends in the price of drugs over the decades of criminalization, wholesale and retail costs of cocaine and heroin have declined sharply as enforcement efforts have intensified. In 1981, the retail cost of 2 g cocaine in a major US city was $545. Twenty years later it was $107. For heroin, the retail (1 g) price was $1,974 in 1981. By 2001, heroin was retailing at $362 for a gram.

The 'iron law of prohibition' explains the increase in drug purity and downward pressure on prices in drug criminalization. The risk of interception of bulky plant products encouraged wholesalers to improve weight-to-value ratios. This is achieved by reducing the size and volume of illicit shipments. Profits are maintained by exporting high purity coca paste and morphine for refining further down the supply chain.

In a 1976 publication on drug markets in Southeast Asia, Joseph Westermeyer observed the 'iron law' in action as post-war opiate criminalization ended a centuries-old, 'public' habit of opium smoking. Users were driven underground and into the shadows. Suppliers responded to prohibition by shifting into the manufacture of more potent heroin. This transformed a once social practice of opium smoking into a surreptitious and risky activity, undertaken out of sight and to maximum immediate effect to reduce the risks of detection, for example by injecting.

Sixty years since countries pledged to eliminate all unauthorized opium poppy cultivation within 15 years, and over a century since activists lobbied against the 'trade in misery', the criminalization of opiates led us to a new stage in the iron law. The synthetic opioid fentanyl, fifty times more powerful than heroin, is now 'easily obtained from the darkweb and transported through the regular mail service', according to Public Safety Canada in 2018.

Another flawed assumption in prohibition thinking relates to the state. When imperial and national representatives attended the Shanghai conference in 1909, the world was a simpler place, dominated by colonial blocks and old empires. Those seeking regulation of opium poppy and coca looked to colonial powers and imperial rulers to restrict cultivation and exports. This assumed a powerful central authority, recognized as sovereign, presiding over neatly demarcated territories, with a functioning bureaucracy, police and the capacity to enforce restrictions on cultivation.

This assumption did not match the complexity of post-war and post-Cold War processes of decolonization, revolution, civil war, independence struggles, or globalization in the 1990s. These historical developments collapsed responsibility for drug plant eradication and export controls to weak post-colonial states with porous borders, ungoverned territories and major problems of poverty and inequality.

The architects of international drug control did not anticipate the phenomenon of weak states – or corrupt states. State institutions and actors are key elements in the illicit drug trade. Drug money permeates politics throughout the world. A multibillion-dollar enterprise could not survive and grow without the participation of government officials, police, civil servants and politicians. The flaw in prohibition thinking and criminalization strategy was to see the state as somehow set apart from the drug trade instead of a main partner.

Prohibition thinking imagined state, market and, as discussed next, individual behaviours that had, and still have, little basis in reality.

Evolving drug-use cultures under criminalization: historical snapshot

Despite the severity of punishment for drug-related offences, censorious social norms, and the risk of adulterated products, people continue using controlled substances without authorization or quality controls. Punitive national criminalization laws have not had a deterrent effect. During the Cold War, an era of global division between the capitalist West and Soviet communism, international drug-control efforts and criminalization strategies were largely confined to the West, where there has been a constant increase in drug use across the decades of criminalization, accelerating as enforcement intensified in the 1980s and 1990s and following the 1988 UN Convention against Illicit Traffic.

The criminalization of the illicit drug trade under the 1961 UN Single Convention incentivized the resurrection of supply chains linking Western consumers to historical plant cultivation zones in former colonies. This ensured ongoing access to substances prohibited under the 1961 Convention and the emergence of new post-war drug cultures. A summary of these trends in the period up to the collapse of Soviet communism is set out next, before moving on to discuss a series of other external shocks to the international drug control system.

Heroin

Illicit heroin demand took off in the US in the 1950s and in Europe in the 1970s, as national restrictions on sales and prescription of opiates were tightened in line with the 1961 UN Single Convention. Initially the key constituency of demand for unauthorized, black-market opiates was established addicts who had previously had access to legal morphine and heroin. In the US, which, as discussed earlier, moved to a criminalization framework in the inter-war period, this constituency was represented by genteel ladies recommended morphine for 'women's problems', and veterans prescribed morphine for battle injuries.

Similarly in Britain, over 80 per cent of narcotic addicts were of 'therapeutic' origin (having become addicted in the course of medical treatment). According to a 1971 study by I. Pierce James, these were mostly women over the age of 50 receiving opiates on prescription, who 'injected themselves in the privacy of their rooms and kept their habit a close secret'.

In 1959 there were 47 registered heroin addicts in the UK. By 1964 this had risen to 328. Heroin use among this demographic was concentrated in London among a new class of non-therapeutic, 'recreational' addicts. According to James, these were 'mostly young (80 per cent male) adults of unstable personality [who] talked of themselves as "junkies"; proclaimed the virtues of "H" and "turned on" their friends [and] formed foci for the epidemic spread of heroin addiction to other younger people who came into contact with them'.

'Macro diffusion' and the seeding of illicit heroin use into new, non-therapeutic user communities occurred on the US East Coast in the 1960s. Heroin epidemics followed the merger of ballooning numbers of small user circles. The profile of the US heroin user changed in this period. A pre-war concentration of illicit use among poor, white urban males shifted to a post-war market of African American and first-generation Latino migrants living in densely populated neighbourhoods blighted by high levels of unemployment, poor housing and poverty. In 1970, heroin overdoses accounted for 100,000 deaths in the US.

Soldiers serving overseas in the new era of Cold War conflicts and decolonization struggles accelerated the embedding of illicit heroin markets. In Australia, which sent 60,000 military to Vietnam between 1962 and 1973, there was increased demand for opiate treatment facilities following repatriation. As the UNODC reported in 2008, 'Even more important, many young US soldiers, who served in Vietnam, came for rest and recreation to Australia, bringing with them their newly acquired drug habits, thus prompting the creation of a cannabis and a heroin market on Australian soil.'

This spilled into the local population and into other Australian territories.

Illicit heroin 'cultures' were associated with a diversity of lifestyles, modes of administration (smoking, snorting and injection), and scenes of use: from the African American jazz movement in the 1930s to New York hipsters and urban squatter groups in West Germany and Switzerland in the 1970s, where heroin use was seen as part of radical alternative, non-conformist lifestyles.

Increased availability of heroin and rising numbers of heroin users in turn led to more injecting behaviours. This was associated with the spread of HIV in the mid-1980s and a popular perception of heroin as a dirty and dangerous drug. In the UK, a 1998 report by Howard Parker and colleagues found that heroin outbreaks 'involved a minority of 18–25-year-olds who were predominantly unemployed and lived in deprived urban areas. Their heroin careers lasted many years, sustained by acquisitive crime, drug dealing and prostitution.'

Despite links to disease spread, death and marginalization, heroin was also reinvented as 'chic'. New heroin cultures in an age of cheaper, purer and more widely available heroin were characterized by 'emaciated, disheveled' fashion models, film actors, and musicians on the 'grunge' guitar-music scene, according to Bryan Denham. The new coolness of heroin was linked to cycles of social change in the context of criminalization. 'Old' and unpopular drugs could regain a foothold if rebranded for a new age, representing a break from preceding drug scenes and cultures. From this perspective, heroin chic was a statement of insularity and rawness, a rejection of the glamour and elitism of the 1980s cocaine scene, and the noisy collectivism of MDMA use and repetitive electronic thud of the rave scene.

At the same time, heroin still continued to be associated with poverty and deprivation. In the UK, distribution networks fanned out into rural and coastal areas, and into younger cohorts of users that Parker and colleagues described in 2004 as the 'socially excluded [...] primarily care leavers, persistent offenders and educational under-achievers who have had impoverished and/or damaged childhoods'.

Cocaine

Heroin remained the most problematic drug in European countries, with the highest level of treatment demand. By contrast in the US, cocaine from Latin America and crack cocaine were a preoccupation. Cocaine powder (cocaine hydrochloride) initially had a limited post-war market; it was expensive, difficult to obtain, and it was not until the mid-1970s that illicit markets re-emerged. These were associated with new club scene cultures in New York, where cocaine was reinvented as a high-end disco drug. As Paul Gootenberg commented in 2001, 'It was popular with 'brainy-sexy types [...] glam rock-stars, Hollywood elites, fun-bent stockbrokers and a jaded post-Nixonian middle-class revved up on the mounting beat of disco'.

Oversupply from Peru, Bolivia and Colombia meant cocaine prices fell, reducing the exclusivity of the drug. Whereas in the early 1970s cocaine barely registered in national surveys of drug use, by 1985 prevalence rates had increased from negligible to 5.1 per cent.

Crack use exploded in New York in 1985. It was sold as a cheap, smokable form of high-end snorted cocaine. It was produced by dissolving powdered cocaine into water and baking soda, boiled until solid and dried into chunks ('rocks'). In a 1986 US Gallup poll, 42 per cent of respondents cited crack and 'other forms of cocaine' as the most serious problem facing the country, ahead of heroin, cannabis and alcohol. By contrast in Europe during the same decade, cocaine was 'still primarily a drug of the upper and the upper-middle classes', and the spread of crack-cocaine was 'still limited' (UNODC 2000).

Box 3.1: Crack cocaine in the US

Unlike snorting cocaine [...] the rewards of the instant high [...] created many repeated episodes of use per day. While heroin users and cocaine snorters may consume their drug two to three times per day, many crack abusers consumed crack five to 15 times per day, limited primarily by their income. (E. Dunlap and B.D. Johnson, in 'The setting for the crack era', 1992)

MDMA and synthetics

Synthetic drugs began to pose an unprecedented challenge in the West in the 1980s with the 'chemical revolution' that combined the empathogen MDMA with new techno-music dance cultures from New York, Detroit and Chicago. Exported to the UK, 'Acid House' morphed into a rave scene that changed the profile of drug users.

A mass-market phenomenon, MDMA mainstreamed recreational drug use, normalizing and democratizing drug taking. MDMA was a 'clean' and simple tab or pill that could be easily concealed and used for non-dependence-inducing 'controlled loss of control', as Fiona Measham put it. The feelings of unity, community and empathy created by the 'love drug' MDMA have been explained as a counter to the social decomposition and individualism associated with Thatcherism and Britain's own experience of neoliberalism in the 1980s.

In 1985, the WHO Expert Committee on Drug Dependence determined that MDMA had no therapeutic application, and the drug was incorporated into Schedule I of the 1971 Convention on Psychotropic Substances. Amendments to national legislative frameworks saw MDMA widely criminalized, alongside new legislation to prevent unregulated raves.

The journey of MDMA from discarded experimental medicine to a most dangerous Schedule I drug with an estimated 20.5 million past year users in the 2020s, parallels the histories of other synthetic drugs such as LSD and amphetamines. Like MDMA, LSD was

Box 3.2: Synthetic drugs, the 'Angels'

The most widely used synthetics in the 2020s were discovered over a century ago, including amphetamine (1887), methamphetamine (1893), MDMA (1912), oxycodone (1916) and LSD (1938).

Synthetics were hailed as wonder drugs, synthetic 'angels', as effective as plant-based 'demon' counterparts, but without risk of dependence in people or on the import of raw plant materials.

German and Japanese distribution of methamphetamine to troops under the brand names Pervitin and Philopon fuelled Allied concerns of Axis military superiority, so US and UK defence sectors accelerated military trials with amphetamines. Benzedrine was routinely distributed to airforce and combat troops.

The wartime experience demonstrated the high abuse potential of methamphetamine and amphetamine, but preference for a more laissez-faire regulatory model prevailed. Light-touch national regulations allowed continued ATS prescription and the development of new 'brain science' medications such as barbiturates and tranquillizers.

Emerging evidence of depression, dependence and suicide associated with the range of synthetic substances culminated in international agreement on tighter controls in the 1971 UN Convention on Psychotropic Substances.

associated with countercultural movements of the period (1960s) and used for mind expansion and exploring the boundaries of reality and consciousness. Both substances demonstrated early positive results in the therapeutic treatment of trauma, depression and anxiety, and the manufacture of both drugs moved underground following their incorporation into the 1971 UN Convention as Schedule I drugs.

Other synthetics that were popularized for a 'high' and which had been introduced as pharmaceutical medicines included amphetamines, which were liberally prescribed in the treatment of depression, obesity and narcolepsy.

The effects of the Smith, Klein & French (SKF) Benzedrine inhaler containing 325 mg of nearly pure amphetamine base were quickly discovered by non-medical users and popularized in jazz circles in the 1930s and among Beatniks in the 1950s. The Beat generation of poets and artists moved on to establish the psychedelic movement and experimentation with LSD and hallucinogens such as peyote and mescaline as amphetamine came under treaty controls in 1971. With criminalization, the trade in amphetamines and amphetamine use were associated with 'speed freaks': biker gangs in North America and Scandinavia, and punks in Europe. At the more benign end of the spectrum, 'speed cultures' were reported among student populations and night workers using amphetamines to boost alertness.

Psychotropics

The autonomy of the pharmaceutical sector under the UN drug treaty system allowed constant innovation to avoid restrictions on clinical research. This included new types of drugs that were intended to rebalance malfunctioning brains and central nervous systems.

For example, sedative barbiturates were initially marketed as an anti-anxiety medication and sleeping aid for the traumatized post-war generation.

A 1956 WHO Expert Committee report found barbiturates to be habit-forming, with a high potential for unsafe dosage. Benzodiazepines (tranquillizers such as Librium and Valium) were quickly popularized by a buoyant post-war advertising industry as a replacement treatment for anxiety, insomnia, professional underperformance, marital conflict and alcohol withdrawal.

Women accounted for twice as many users of tranquillizers as men, with high rates of dependence and side effects that included suicidal thoughts. These problems were not stigmatized in the same way as 'hard drug' use, which was associated with young men, delinquency, deviance and self-inflicted harm. Tranquillizer dependence evoked widespread public sympathy for addicted users. Pharmaceutical companies were encouraged to improve the performance of anti-anxiety medications which led to the introduction of selective serotonin reuptake inhibitors (SSRIs).

In 1987, Eli Lilly received approval from the US Food and Drug Administration for fluoxetine, which came onto the market in 1988 under the trade name Prozac.

Following what Mickey Smith in 1991 termed the 'law of the wonder drug' associated with previous 'blockbuster medicines', Prozac went through the three steps of: wild media hype and mass marketing; overprescription and overuse; and identification of dependence problems and clinical review.

This was the picture in the West as the Cold War was coming to an end, with the world and economic markets on the edge of global integration processes. Illicit drug markets had thrived under Western criminalization regimes, cannabis in particular. Despite federal laws in the US introducing mandatory sentences for cannabis-related offences in the 1950s, cannabis cultivation and use prevailed. Cannabis subcultures also embedded in Australia and in European countries such as the UK and France. This fused countercultural, migrant, intellectual and musical streams around the rituals and symbols of cannabis. User numbers were resilient despite stricter laws and harsher enforcement regimes in the 1970s and 1980s.

When the Berlin Wall collapsed in 1989, opening the countries of the Soviet bloc to the West, it transpired that cannabis and other illicit drug markets had also been thriving in the insular Soviet states, despite intense denial by national communist parties and Soviet leadership in Moscow.

External shocks and unwelcome surprises: globalization and drug-market convergence

Much of Southern Europe (Spain, Greece and Portugal), Latin America, Southeast Asia and Africa were isolated in the post-war period by varieties of authoritarian, fascist and apartheid rule. Pervasive social and police surveillance snuffed out opportunities for using substances such as cannabis, LSD, cocaine and heroin that were popular in the West.

Things did begin to change following the Soviet invasion of Afghanistan in 1979, which exposed Soviet troops to Afghan opiates and the trade in cannabis from Central Asia. As with the experience of US and Australian personnel serving in conflicts in the Southeast Asian 'golden triangle', many returned with problems of heroin dependence or addiction.

New supply chains opened to serve burgeoning heroin demand that by the mid-1980s extended to Soviet satellite states such as Poland, where per capita opiate use approximated rates in the West, most people using homemade, injectable *kompot*, manufactured from household chemicals and poppy stalk.

The end of the Cold War and transitions from authoritarianism saw the end of controls on economic and civic life. New personal and collective freedoms, the decline of censorship, and private sector entrepreneurialism drove cultural globalization, or 'McDonaldization', according to George Ritzer (in 1993). This included the import of Western fashion, music and nightlife scenes associated with the use of drugs.

External suppliers were eager to exploit new drug-market openings in transition countries. Old and new local crime groups, many incorporating police, bureaucrats and security officials from the authoritarian period, were open to novel transcontinental partnerships, for example linking Albanian and Bulgarian crime networks to Bolivian and Mexican suppliers. In Russia the Ministry of Internal Affairs estimated over 5,000 Organized Crime Groups (OCGs) operated in the country, with 100,000 members in 1993. In Poland, the number of OCGs increased from 26 in 1994 to 731 in 1997.

Neoliberal policies that aimed to shift insular, state-centric economies to dynamic growth (and debt repayment) through a combination of public spending cuts, free trade and integration into regional and global markets smoothed the globalization of illicit drug markets. Free movement of goods, money and people expanded options for drug supply routes and transportation of larger shipments of drugs through now poorly policed frontiers. Airfares halved between 1980 and 2005 enabling market entry by small-scale traffickers and eroding the model of hierarchical, large-scale drug supply organizations.

Chaotic and opaque financial liberalization and privatization processes in transition countries facilitated the washing of illicit revenues, for example through the purchase of state assets such as ports, airports, banks, land and mining concessions.

Global openings also provided access to precursor chemicals for synthetic drug manufacture from newly accessible industrial producers such as China and India.

Following China's open-door policy and economic reform, illicit drugs quickly returned, starting in the southwest province of Yunnan bordering Myanmar. HIV infection among injecting heroin users in Yunnan was reported in the late 1980s. By 1995, infection had increased in Sichuan and Xinjiang Provinces. The Chinese Communist Party responded with statements of denial. Weak epidemiological surveillance of disease obscured the vulnerability of authoritarian states to HIV/AIDS linked to injecting drug use. This broke forcefully in the mid-1990s, with a fivefold increase in HIV cases between 1995 and 1997. In 1999, Karl Dehne and colleagues found that 90 per cent of cases were concentrated in Ukraine, Russia and Belarus.

International drug control was ill positioned to contain either globalized drug markets or the increase in consumer markets following the collapse of the Soviet bloc and the liberalization processes that this unleashed. Consumer demand grew strongly in the transition countries and alongside the export of Western criminalization strategies that had failed to contain drug market growth in the West. Here it is worth highlighting another external shock that has made the ambitions of international drug control even more difficult to achieve in the modern age: technological change.

Technological change

The internet, mobile telephony, digital currencies, encryption and new plant-growing and drone technologies are transforming the way people cultivate, move, manufacture, sell and procure illicit drugs and how they communicate and pay for these activities. This makes it harder for national authorities to prevent people from obtaining drugs and drug-related information, and it requires new policing and enforcement skills.

The first online cannabis transaction was purportedly in 1971, involving students at Stanford University and Massachusetts Institute of Technology using US Department of Defense ARPANET accounts (Advanced Research Projects Agency Network), the forerunner of the internet. When the first web browsers were launched, user groups set up online forums for information exchange, moving into commercial online sale of substances, equipment and paraphernalia by the end of the 1990s.

Traceable payment systems were a liability. In the 2000s, transactions migrated to the invisible and anonymous darknet. This was made possible by the (downloadable) availability of Tor software, created in 2002 in a US Department of Defense project. Innovation in encryption and cryptocurrencies accelerated a shift to large 'public' online drug markets such as Silk Road.

Launched in 2011, Silk Road took payment in bitcoin and made drug transactions 'as easy as buying used electronics—and seemingly as safe. It's Amazon—if

Amazon sold mind-altering chemicals', as Adrian Chen wrote in *Wired* in 2011. By 2013 the number of user accounts had increased from an opening 130 to almost a million. Silk Road was shut down in a 2013 law enforcement operation. A raft of new darknet market ventures moved into the vacuum. Silk Road 2.0 opened less than a month later.

At an estimated annual US$700 million, the value of darknet drug transactions in 2020 was modest. Markets are largely the recourse of English-speaking, non-chaotic drug users (the number of heroin-related transactions is low) and concentrated around cannabis (a third of sales), cocaine, amphetamine, MDMA and psychedelics.

The importance of darknet markets is the capacity for growth driven by the uptake of new digital skills by buyers and sellers. The UNODC noted in 2021 that while darknet drug commerce accounts for a fraction of illicit drug market sales, 'the trend is upward'. Digital drug transactions do not involve the risks associated with open street markets, lowering entry barriers for new users and retailers, including women. With customer forums providing star ratings, profit relies on good customer service, quality of product, reliability of delivery, and transaction security. This places a premium on the same capital skills requirements of mainstream businesses and creates competing employment opportunities. Darknet markets are in turn being challenged by social media dealing, and the use of encrypted messaging apps that sprung up during COVID-19 lockdown.

In 2020, lockdown brought a 'golden age' for online drug sales despite initial delivery disruptions, suggesting consumers adapted quickly both to digital technologies and changing drug-demand needs. A British report in 2021 by the organization Release with information gathered from 2,621 survey respondents during this period of extreme state surveillance (9 April–17 September 2020) found that supply of the preferred drug was not interrupted, more people were becoming digitally literate and taking to online purchasing, and physical exchanges adhered to government-advised social distancing measures.

Respondents also reported an increase in their drug use and available choices. Preferences did change, away from the more social stimulant drugs such as cocaine, amphetamine and MDMA, in favour of cannabis and increasingly the benzodiazepine medications.

The international marketplace

Globalization, neoliberalism, technological shift and other forms of social change that have occurred outside the control of the international drug control regime, and largely unanticipated by its institutions, have reshaped the illicit drug trade of the 2000s.

The historic classification of states as either 'consumer', 'supply', or 'trafficking' countries has collapsed, with all three activities now occurring at some level in most countries. Drugs are no longer imported from faraway countries but are increasingly domestically cultivated and manufactured. Illicit drug use is no longer a fringe activity among sub-populations in the West, but a 'global habit', according to Paul Stares in 1999, as traditional 'supply', 'trafficking' and insulated states in the Global South have developed large consumer markets. Payment in drugs for access and secure transit through countries has increased the availability of heroin and cocaine in the 'trampoline' states of Central America, the Caribbean, East and West Africa, and Central Europe that bounce drugs forward along supply chains. The synthetic drug revolution and local manufacture of amphetamine, methamphetamine and opioids has added to a crowded and diverse market of available substances and consumer choice.

Access to a greater suite of plant-based and synthetic drugs is changing user cultures in the developed drug markets of the Global North, and as discussed in Chapter 1 in relation to injecting drug use and risky behaviours. This includes polydrug use – combining drug types to alter or prolong psychological and/or physiological sensation; 'chemsex', defined by Hannah McCall and colleagues in 2015 as 'intentional sex under the influence of psychoactive drugs, mostly among men who have sex with men […] to facilitate sexual sessions lasting several hours or days with multiple sexual partners'; and 'microdosing' with very low doses of psychedelics to improve mental health and wellbeing.

Just as the divide between 'producer' and 'consumer' countries has given way to integrated and globalized drug markets, traditional gender divisions in consumption are being eroded. In 2018, women accounted for one third of drug users globally and one fifth of injecting drug users, according to UNODC's *World Drug Report* for that year. There is a lack of research on women's drug use experiences, motivations and behaviours, and this is revealed in the major gaps in treatment provision and overcrowding of prison facilities.

> **Box 3.3: Gender in drug policy**
>
> As we saw in Chapter 2, early campaigners argued that prohibiting narcotics (and alcohol) was a progressive intervention to protect women and girls. This discourse framed women as passive and vulnerable victims of the drug trade, a gendered construct that remained influential.
>
> From the early 1900s through to second wave feminism in the 1960s, women users of 'hard' drugs were seen as victims of male power, with initiation into drug use mediated by men and maintained through exploitative transactions such as sex work.
>
> Seen as lacking in 'subcultural capital' and focused on their role as caregivers, women's interaction with illicit markets was of peripheral interest to policy-making, clinical and policing concern.
>
> The lack of interest in women's drug use and illicit drug market participation extended to academia. Trysh Travis complained in 2019 that 'Academic feminists in humanities and social science have shown themselves curiously reluctant to historicize, theorize, or otherwise mount complex investigations of women's substance use and/or cessation'.

New drug use practices, settings, and types of drugs in the policy setting of criminalization require new forms of treatment, harm reduction and drug education. Few countries are responding to the urgency of these challenges or addressing the new forms of health risk and crime with which the use of some of these substances can be associated.

One example is the depressant GHB (Gamma-Hydroxybutyrate), which has relaxant and sedative effects. Legally available as a sleeping aid in the 1990s and now widely available online, GHB is popular in niche club and party scenes, for example in the community of men who have sex with men (MSM).

Overdose is easy and can lead to a loss of consciousness. In this context, GHB is also notorious as a 'date rape' drug linked to non-consensual sexual acts. As with all drugs, education and treatment lag far behind the accumulation of drug-related harms. The obstacles to awareness raising and safe use remain the same: stigma and fear of criminal prosecution for possession or use.

The limits of deterrence

Discussions on chemsex are no doubt far from where US delegates to the 1909 Shanghai Opium Conference imagined the world would be six decades into a universal drug prohibition.

This chapter has so far explored the conditions that have enabled how drug demand and cultures have changed and proliferated over the decades of criminalization. This final section outlines other explanations for continued high demand, and the reasons people are not deterred from using banned and sometimes adulterated substances.

Pleasure and pain

People continue to use drugs because drugs are pleasurable. This pleasure comes from the effects of the substance and the social contexts and rituals of use. Types of pleasure (and its intensity) are subjective and range from the sexual energy associated with some stimulant drugs, to the mind exploration and other-worldliness of psychedelics, or to the wellbeing emphasis of cannabis use and microdosing.

The concept of drug use as pleasurable is unconscionable in the UN drug treaties. The treaties explicitly prohibit 'recreational' use. This results in a mismatch between policy expectations of deterrence and the experience of users.

Beyond pleasure, people continue to rely on illicit substances for the relief from mental or physical pain: public health systems are failing to address chronic and debilitating illnesses and treatment needs.

Discredited drug laws

Drug use continues under criminalization because criminalization has lost credibility. Draconian sentencing regimes for drug-related offences have not delivered positive results. Drug laws that are exemplary and disproportionate do not command social legitimacy (as the Organization of American States (OAS) report in 2013 on the drug problem in the Americas found).

Long-documented problems of racist enforcement of drug laws and police focus on 'easily' arrestable populations (for example homeless people) has contributed to huge growth of the prison population. The 'warehousing' of prisoners in large-scale detention facilities is distant from the 'rehabilitative' ideal in criminal justice systems and notions of reforming and rehabilitating offenders.

Prisoners lack access to drug or other treatments, and to training, education and post-release support. This has had criminogenic outcomes, including high rates of repeat offending, the acceleration of substance problems within and outside of prison, and strengthened offender networks.

These consequences are visible to publics globally and undermine the credibility of drug laws: 'Like the crime it is supposed to deal with, punishment is nowadays seen as a chronic social problem' (as David Garland observed in 1990).

Treatment failings

As previously stated, most people who use drugs do so without adverse health or other consequences. This is not the case for about a tenth of users. The 1961 UN Single Convention encourages states to provide 'measures of treatment, education, after-care, rehabilitation, and social reintegration'. This has not translated into appropriate and properly funded care, which itself is a violation of the right to health, or participation in treatment programme design and monitoring of those people who have used drugs problematically or continue to do so. This contravenes Human Rights-Based Approaches. The neglect of treatment demand and the failure of states globally to provide accessible, appropriate and well-resourced support for people who use harmfully perpetuates high rates of relapse and problematic use.

There is a serious global problem of underfunded treatment services, with anti-drug budgets and donor funding absorbed by law enforcement and the criminal justice system. Where services are available, criminalization has built stigma and police violence into the lives of drug-using communities. This is a major barrier to access. As the UNODC conceded in 2008, 'A system appears to have been created in which those who fall into the web of addiction find themselves excluded and marginalized from the social mainstream, tainted with a moral stigma, and often unable to find treatment even when motivated to seek it'.

Box 3.4: Rose, II

In my 2020 interview with Rose, in which we discussed the death of her two sons, Roland and Jake, she talked about Roland's plans to go to college:

> So he went to try and get treatment and was put on a waiting list for a methadone programme. He was

doing his best, staying at home as much as he could. He asked us to look after him, to help him. The treatment service told him he needed to reduce his heroin use and they would keep testing him before he could get onto the programme. We discussed this and I said to him, 'I think I need to take control, take control of you,' so what we agreed was I would give him the money for the heroin – I would at least have some control. I knew he would not be taking money out of my handbag, stealing things from the house – that had happened before. I felt at least I was taking charge.

We agreed on a set amount of money that I would give him to buy heroin. I would go with him – as near as he would allow to the place where he was going to get the heroin. He would give it straight to me, I would hide it and then dole it out to him at regular intervals. I knew it was against the law. I knew what I was doing was illegal, but I was more concerned about helping him.

After he had been waiting six weeks to get onto the methadone programme, one of his friends phoned and said their parents were away and he was having friends around.

Roland died of an overdose at the party.

The policeman said to me that it had all come out that I had been giving Roland heroin so I would have to be questioned at the police station. So there I was, grieving for Roland and worrying at the same time about this

> forthcoming interview. I did not know if they would put me in jail for supply. Six months went by before they called me for the formal interview. So that was another anxiety gnawing at me for all that time. When the interview came, it was a lot of questioning. Then I was told it would not be taken any further.

Inappropriate treatment services sustain problematic consumption. There is a lack of choice in treatment settings, with provision dominated by abstinence-based therapies with a strongly spiritual element. Faith can be important in recovery, but the proliferation of faith-based 'cure' missions in places such as Latin America and East Africa has raised concerns about harmful and abusive practices. Most abstinence-based facilities receive public (and private) funding and have commercial (and personal) interests in political lobbying and popular mobilization to restrict service provision to abstinence programmes.

Box 3.5: Happy, I

In 2020, Happy, an activist from Tanzania in the International Network of People who Use Drugs (INPUD), told me about their experience of faith-based groups:

> They closed all of drop-in centres for LGBTI communities, even ours .... Peer services are very helpful – rather than going to a stranger and explaining your sicknesses

> and then having them pull out a Bible or a Koran and saying, 'this verse says you are wrong'. I know maybe I might be wrong, but who knows if you are right? We are not here to point fingers. I've come here to have this service provided to me. If I need the Bible, I'll go to the church. If I need the Koran, I'll go to the mosque.

Abstinence is not achievable for all users. This is acknowledged in harm reduction and 'maintenance' programmes, for example that provide opioid substitution therapies such as oral methadone and buprenorphine. The 'British System' of pure pharmaceutical heroin prescription to patients that was largely abandoned in the UK in the 1960s (because of the non-therapeutic demand highlighted earlier in the work of James) is offered to people for whom abstinence and other therapies have not worked in countries including Germany, Switzerland, the Netherlands and Denmark. Alternative treatment approaches are underfunded and face criticism that they are enabling drug use.

The disease model of addiction has dominated clinical and psychiatric practice and policy-making circles for decades. Addiction is defined as a behavioural disorder induced by a drug 'hijacking' the brain, triggering neurological abnormalities. This theory informs many abstinence-based approaches and clinical research into brain 'medicines'.

> **Box 3.6: Suzanne, II**
>
> In 2020, I interviewed Suzanne for the edited collection *The Impact of Global Drug Policy on Women*. Discussing her own experience of drug and alcohol treatment, she said:
>
> > I relapsed so I got chucked out. That is what I don't understand. If you go into hospital for a heart attack, you have all this treatment – but if you have another heart attack you would get kicked out? Problematic substance use is the only illness where this happens. To relapse and get chucked out is really harsh. All that did for me was reconfirm I am a complete failure, a bad person, that I did not deserve my children, they were better off without me. I was given ten minutes to pack my bags, and a train ticket. I just remember going shoplifting and then home. But I could not go 'home' as I had used up all my chances with my family.

Critics of 'brain theories' argue these models lack scientific rigour, diminish the agency and choices of people who use drugs, and ignore complex psychosocial and environmental factors such as poverty, marginalization, racism and trauma that mediate experiences of addiction.

As for legitimate demand and improved access to essential medicines and substances that improve physical and mental health, strict regulatory requirements for the storage, handling and prescription of Schedule I/

Class A drugs impedes clinical research, for example on psychedelic therapies, and the storing of analgesic opiates for pain relief and end-of-life care across the world. Most low- and middle-income countries do not engage with the complex, bureaucratic process of estimating essential medicine requirements for the following year and submitting requests to the scrutiny of the International Narcotics Control Board.

This situation has sustained a 'global pain crisis'. The 2021 UNODC *World Drug Report* declared: 'In 2019, four standard doses of controlled pain medication were available every day for every one million inhabitants in West and Central Africa, in comparison to 32,000 doses in North America.'

Drug control strategy is lopsided, locked into policing, punishment, prisons and abstinence. This is inappropriate for addressing contemporary user trends, and the more complex profiles of user patterns and treatment needs. Demand-side responses address the manifestations of drug use, not the cause. Deterrence at the core of drug control strategy is rooted in assumptions about individual user behaviours and motivations that are outdated or unevidenced, which have been proven wrong over time, and which have informed interventions counterproductive for the goal of preventing unauthorised substance use. As discussed in the next chapter, the same problem exists on the supply side of the drug policy equation.

4
THE PROBLEM OF ENDLESS SUPPLY

Let's have a quick recap. So far it has been argued that our contemporary drug policies are rooted in the prejudices and great power conflicts of the 1900s, that the post-war turn to criminalization was premised on mistaken assumptions about how states, markets and individuals would behave under a drug prohibition, and that strategy and metrics have been preoccupied with the manifestations of a buoyant illicit drug market and not its causes.

The previous chapter discussed how this has resulted in unbalanced and misguided interventions that have failed to reduce drug consumption and harmful drug-related behaviours. If demand-side strategies have underperformed, what does the situation look like on the supply side?

As the data in Chapter 1 demonstrate, the answer is not very well. The 1961 UN Single Convention set out a maximum 25-year timeframe for the elimination of all unauthorized drug plant cultivation. In the 2020s, over sixty years later, coca and opium poppy farming is at record highs.

Unfortunately – if not inevitably – we see a mirror image of policy and enforcement failings. Just as people have continued to use illicit substances irrespective of the risk of punishment, so farmers of coca, opium poppy and cannabis have continued to harvest these crops, despite the threat of arrest and crop eradication by state security forces. And more people are involved in manufacture, trafficking and drug distribution activities. Criminalization has not reduced illicit drug supply volumes or the numbers of illicit drug suppliers. It appears to proliferate them.

A war on plants

As discussed in Chapter 2, the US was long preoccupied with ending the legal agricultural trade in the opium poppy, coca and cannabis plants. A ban on cultivation required 'little sacrifice from Americans while demanding fundamental social and institutional change from others,' writes William McAllister in his 1999 exposition of US 'narcodiplomacy'.

Agitation by the prohibition lobby to curtail opium poppy cultivation in British colonial territories in the 1880s and 1890s was rebuffed by British officials. In British-administered India, a Crown agent observed, 'Owing to the system of advances and the large amount of ready money brought into the villages, poppy cultivation will always be looked upon as advantageous.' There was always a market for opium poppy, 'which commands a steady price'.

An official in Burma set out that such a move would be 'undesirable because opium is the main source of livelihood in many parts of the Shan States'. Any restrictions would require the whole region to be taken under direct administration 'entailing armed interference on a large scale'. The cost 'would be enormous and unremunerative'. The US Judd Resolution of 1944 brushed away these concerns. It expressed 'the conviction of the Congress that this World War ought to be not an occasion for permitting expansion and spreading of illicit traffic in opium but rather an opportunity for completely eliminating it'.

Having achieved international agreement that unauthorized cultivation should be criminalized and illicit crops eradicated in the 1961 UN Single Convention, the US moved quickly to support implementation of the ban in cultivating countries. This source-focused approach, eradicating and interdicting drugs before they arrive on US shores, has been a key characteristic of US strategy over the decades. The 1961 Convention did not provide compensation to farmers or national economies that had relied on the revenues made from trading plants that had now been prohibited. The US used 'narcodiplomacy' to convince governments with cultivation zones to forfeit an important agricultural sector and align with the post-war control regime.

Turkey and Iran were the first to be shepherded towards an opium poppy ban. Trade agreements, financial aid and the opportunity to cultivate low-level amounts for legal UN quotas were offered by US officials in exchange for an opium poppy prohibition. There were also threats of sanctions. Government prohibitions were issued and rescinded in the 1950s, 1960s and 1970s amid destabilizing cycles of protest and nationalist, anti-American agitation.

The Mexican government began cannabis eradication in 1971 following intense pressure from the US, including a two-month border closure in 1969. With the launch of the first major bilateral US–Mexican anti-drug agreement, Operation Condor, in 1975, mass spraying with Paraquat began in Mexico, supported by $30 million US funding and the provision of 39 spray helicopters and 22 reconnaissance planes.

The route of legal, if diminished, cultivation was also offered to Latin American coca-cultivating communities. The UN permitted state monopolies in Peru and Bolivia to oversee coca farming to a fixed quota for domestic 'quasi-medical' use in indigenous practices.

The US generally abjured engaging directly with the source of the problem, farmers and rural poverty, preferring instead to provide development assistance funding to opaque, corrupt and repressive central governments. US financial aid for rural transitions out of poppy, coca and cannabis farming was modest, misdirected and vastly outstripped by funding for foreign police, military and other counternarcotics actors. There were some discrete small-scale development projects associated with the

US development agency USAID. These provided seeds, fertilizer and agricultural equipment to cultivators, with the aim of encouraging licit farming of commodities such as fruit, tobacco, nuts, wheat and vegetables.

From the 1960s through to the 1990s, US-funded and usually USAID-delivered crop substitution initiatives were rolled out in opium poppy areas in Pakistan, Laos, Mexico, Myanmar; in coca cultivation zones in Peru, Bolivia and Colombia; and in cannabis cultivation zones in Lebanon and Morocco. The results were endlessly disappointing. A 1996 US Government Accountability Office report on funding for UN initiatives in Myanmar found that crop substitution projects 'have been largely ineffective, since they have been too small in scope, were inadequately planned, and have not gained support from the Burmese government'.

There was also opposition within some sections of US federal government to funding for cultivators until there was proof all farming had been permanently terminated. This created tremendous economic stress for households during the transition between destroying plants, qualifying for assistance and alternative crops progressing through the cycle of planting, harvesting and marketing.

The lack of progress encouraged the US to pivot to more aggressive source-focused containment efforts. As outlined by Reagan in 1982, 'We're rejecting the helpless attitude that drug use is so rampant that we're defenceless to do anything about it [...] We can fight the drug problem, and we can win.'

Backed by US Congressional approval of a $38 million budget for anti-drug efforts overseas, and new powers to decertify countries deemed non-compliant with US control efforts, President Reagan launched a new phase of militarized anti-drug efforts in source countries, which focused on Mexico and Latin America. Warfare reframed cultivators as 'criminal' actors and legitimate targets of offensive operations such as crop-spraying exercises and land clearances. This repressive approach adopted by Reagan was continued by Republican and Democratic Party successors.

US-sponsored crop eradication and drug interdiction campaigns provided capacity-building and technical and financial support to Latin American militaries. Offensive operations in this new and violent drug war were launched in Bolivia, starting with Operation Blast Furnace in 1986, followed by Peru (Andean Strategy, 1989), Colombia (Plan Colombia, 1998), Mexico and Central America (Mérida Initiative, or Plan Mexico, 2007) and Central America (the Central America Regional Security Initiative, 2008). These have been costly source containment campaigns for the US taxpayer.

The initial layout for Plan Colombia, for example, was $1.3 billion and had reached over $10 billion by 2015. Plan Mexico absorbed $3 billion of US funding. The Central America Regional Security Initiative (CARSI) (2008–12) provided $2.8 billion of US weapons and radar equipment to Belize, Costa Rica, El Salvador, Guatemala, Honduras, Nicaragua and Panama, and defence contracts worth $67 million.

CARSI also involved the deployment of 4,000 US troops in counternarcotics operations, including the Fourth Fleet in the Caribbean, the National Guard in Honduras and 200 marines on the Guatemalan coast under Operation Martillo.

These programmes have not been successful in reducing drug plant cultivation or the flow of drugs. Recipient countries have also been expected to pick up shortfalls in law enforcement spending to police US priorities. The OAS in 2013 reported that this has diverted public revenues from development initiatives that 'plausibly have particularly high returns in lower income countries, suggesting that the opportunity costs of drug enforcement per dollar spent may be particularly high in countries where the needs for poverty alleviation programs and public investments are acute'.

There was also an accumulation of evidence that US-sponsored forced eradication exercises and the presence of military and paramilitary forces have had negative consequences for rural farmers. This included displacement from homes and communities, and horrific human rights violations such as extrajudicial executions, rapes, arbitrary detentions and forced disappearances.

Militarized campaigns did not strengthen the legitimacy or the coercive capacity of weak states in drug crop cultivation zones, and they exposed soldiers to opportunities for corruption and bribery to prevent or encourage eradication exercises. External support for the security sector, and strategies of strengthening the coercive state, exacerbated existing legacies of state impunity and violence in regional contexts such as Latin and Central America. There was also limited progress containing cultivation levels. State violence simply displaced farming households: it did not address their reliance on illicit agricultural farming.

> **Box 4.1: Fumigation costs**
>
> In a chapter contributed to the 2020 edited collection, *The Impact of Global Drug Policy and Women*, Isabel Pereira and Lucía Ramírez included interviews with women in coca-growing areas of Colombia. One interviewee, Gloria, told them:
>
>> [In 2000], they sprayed our crops. It was awful. They sprayed the pasture, our cassava, plantain, corn, rice. It was something we didn't expect – to be left with bunches of plantains that are damaged ... We were left without food. My husband had to go find work somewhere else in order to buy us food.

Development approaches in drug control

As acknowledged in the landmark 'Action Plan on International Cooperation on the Eradication of Illicit Drug Crops and on Alternative Development' produced by the 1998 United Nations General Assembly Special Session on Drugs (UNGASS), 'Despite the adoption of international conventions promoting the prohibition of illicit drug crops, the problem of the illicit cultivation of the opium poppy, the coca bush and the cannabis plant continues at alarming levels.' The action plan defined alternative development (AD) as 'a process to prevent and eliminate the illicit cultivation of plants [...] through specifically designed rural development measures'. Development-led responses were acknowledged to be 'an important component for generating and promoting lawful, viable and sustainable economic options to illicit drug crop cultivation'.

The softer, development-focused approach was taken by EU governments and UN agencies such as the United Nations Development Programme (UNDP) and supported by regional bodies such as the OAS. AD emphasized non-coercive, holistic interventions beyond simple crop substitution projects, and programmes that addressed the causes of reliance on illicit crops and decisions to cultivate, such as poverty or lack of access to land and formal markets.

AD initiatives addressed a major gap in the international drug control regime, which had no mandate, agencies or money to respond to country requests for development support. At the same time, cultivators and cultivating countries were neglected by development agencies.

A 2019 report by Christian Aid reflected on illicit drug economies as a 'blind spot' for the development community, which was dominated by the conventional view that drug crop economies 'lie

Box 4.2: Alternative development: the Thailand model

Alternative development was influenced by projects in Thailand to reduce opium poppy cultivation in the country's Northern Highlands. From 1965 to 1994, these were successful in shrinking the area under opium poppy cultivation by 88 per cent.

The Thai royal family were influential in steering the country away from its status as a 'Golden Triangle' heroin hub. King Bhumibol Adulyadej's Thai Royal Highlands Project (RHP) and (after 1988) the Princess Mother Mae Fah Luang Foundation's Doi Tung Development Project engaged directly with Hmong opium poppy cultivators displaced from Maoist China to Thailand's northern borderlands.

Lack of official papers, economic opportunities and access to education, banking and health care were identified as sustaining reliance on opium poppy planting. This was addressed by donor (mainly German) and Thai state investment in citizenship and services agreed with cultivating communities.

To avoid economic stress on Hmong farmers during this transition, opium poppy was only eradicated when alternative incomes were in place and the presence of the state was secured. Opium smoking continued to be permitted.

outside the development sphere', and were a type of 'distortion or pathology that must be isolated, combatted and destroyed'. AD aimed to reverse this siloing of cultivating territories and integrate them into national development, peacebuilding and poverty reduction strategies.

This approach aligned international drug control with the intellectual shifts of the 2000s and the embrace of the 'human security' paradigm by the United Nations. This emphasized an international order based on human rights obligations and serving the security needs of individuals. These were broadly defined: for example, a world free from hunger, poverty and disease. The UN 2000 Millennium Development Goals and 2030 Agenda for Sustainable Development reflect this lean away from 'hard security' and singular concern with the security of nation states. It appeared that these were propitious times for development-led initiatives to reduce the age-old problem of opium poppy, coca and cannabis supply, and at a time when synthetic drugs were also becoming a major challenge for the international drug control system.

Traction under development-oriented responses to drug crop cultivation was dissipated by the countervailing force of militarization as counterterrorism and counternarcotics elided in the US 'war on terror' of the early 2000s in contexts such as Afghanistan and Colombia.

The limits of 'alternative' and 'development'

Development-focused initiatives drastically underperformed. These programmes suffered a severe shortfall in funding as multilateral and bilateral assistance programmes were refocused on policing, the military and criminal justice systems. In 2017, funding for AD was US$275 million, equivalent to 0.1 per cent of global funding for development cooperation. According to German international development agency, BMZ, in 2020: 'By contrast, the revenues of international drug trafficking networks are estimated to amount to between $426 and $652 billion.'

AD programming experienced other implementation challenges, including the capture of resources by community gatekeepers, warlords and predatory agro-industrial interests looking to clear land of legitimate and illicit small-scale farmers.

On an operational level, divisions persisted between (US-backed) military and (EU-sponsored) development actors and strategies. The US remained hostile to projects such as road building and transportation, which are integral to AD. In the opinion of the US, these investments facilitated drug trafficking and the movement of insurgents in and out of cultivation territories.

Poor communications and fragmented programming were also a problem for AD, and more ambitious Development-Oriented Drug Control interventions that were devised by BMZ.

The US Special Inspector General for Afghanistan Reconstruction (SIGAR) found in 2018: 'Everyone did their own thing, not thinking how it fitted in with the larger effort. The state was trying to eradicate, USAID was marginally trying to do livelihoods, and DEA was going after bad guys'. A review of UK development assistance to Afghanistan highlighted the lack of sustainability and financial transparency in AD programmes, insensitivity in design processes, and lack of consultation with impacted communities.

Trade agreements that were presented as AD frequently made the economic situation of cultivating communities *and* countries worse. For example in the US, the Andean Trade Preference Act (ATPA) of 1991 promised to assist Colombia, Bolivia, Peru and Ecuador to reduce reliance on cocaine exports by generating alternative economic opportunities such as manufacturing. Duty-free access to the US for selected goods allowed the four Andean countries to triple exports to the US from $9.6 billion in 2002 to $28.9 billion by 2010. This did not translate into employment opportunities for plant cultivators, though. The main US imports were petroleum products, tin, silver, coal, copper and gold. The ATPA, and its successor, the ATPDEA (Andean Trade Promotion and Drug Eradication Act of 2002), also required that Andean countries reciprocate US tariff reductions. This led to a doubling of US exports, from $6.46 billion in 2002 to $11.64 billion by 2006, contributing to job losses.

Eradication failures explained: the importance of drug crops

Efforts to stop unauthorized drug plant cultivation with coercive state force have been well funded and relentless for at least the past 60 years. At the same time, we have record levels of illicit cultivation in the 2020s, 115 years since US President Roosevelt convened the Shanghai opium conference and global powers began the quest to limit cultivation strictly to medical need only.

The simplest explanation for the failure to get anywhere near ambitions of zero drug plant cultivation is that plants such as opium poppy, coca and cannabis play a multifunctional role in the lives of vulnerable households. These conditions and the security that is provided by illicit cultivation have not been addressed or ameliorated by militarized responses or AD initiatives.

Cultivation zones have remained zones of multidimensional poverty, with high levels of insecurity, conflict and land poverty. They are typically remote, peripheral and outside the purview, services and security of the state.

Opium poppy, coca and cannabis farming is the best of limited options for the land poor, the displaced and households suffering other forms of economic stress, for example triggered by violent conflict, a collapse in the market for legal agricultural goods, or unemployment and dispossession associated with the privatization of land, industry and infrastructure during neoliberal adjustments to national economies.

These are resilient cash crops, providing regular harvests in arduous environments, with guaranteed markets and intermediary purchasers of harvested plant materials. The comparatively speedy growth cycle (120 days from planting to harvest in the case of opium poppy) and durability (30 years of harvest per coca bush) make cultivation propitious in contexts of land insecurity and eradication risks. In contrast to alternative, licit agricultures such as apples, peppers or coffee that drug plant farmers are encouraged (and coerced) to move into, coca and opium poppy are less vulnerable to pests and disease, and do not require large areas of land or irrigation for planting, or facilities for storage or refrigeration. Input costs are low and plant products are durable and can be stored. This enables farmers to maximize income by holding back sales until prices improve. The high value-to-weight ratio of coca, cannabis and opium poppy renders small levels of cultivation profitable.

UNODC figures from 2018 estimate 605,000–970,000 households worldwide were engaged in illicit opium poppy and coca farming. In Bolivia, a fifth of the workforce found employment in the coca sector after the collapse of tin markets and a searing process of economic liberalization in the 1980s.

Martin Jelsma links the growth of Colombian opium poppy cultivation in the early 1990s to the end of the International Coffee Agreement (ICA) in 1989. This had guaranteed minimum incomes to coffee farmers, impacting the livelihoods of an estimated 350,000 small coffee producers in Latin America.

In Morocco, 'For the Rifan farmer cannabis represented an opportunity to move rapidly from a subsistence family economy to a cash economy: precarious, certainly, but substantial'. In South Africa:

> The producers of dagga (cannabis) are an army of small farmers, mostly poor and black, who supplement their subsistence agriculture with a patch of easy-to-grow cash crop [...] These rural producers are not part of some massive drug conspiracy; they earn money for school fees, transportation costs or other activities where cash is required.

In Afghanistan, the opium economy constituted 'a well-linked market in terms of credit, purchase, transport and processing', with five jobs generated in the rural non-farm economy for each hectare of opium poppy cultivated, according to research by David Mansfield and Adam Paine.

Security considerations are also influential in decisions to plant. Again, as with the livelihood element of cultivation, this has not been addressed in anti-drug programming. In territories where the state presence is weak or hostile, criminal entrepreneurs, bandits and warlords provide public goods and physical protection for cultivators and their crops, and negotiate cultivator access to market, capital and land.

Illicit planting is also a highly risky strategy for sustaining livelihoods and guaranteeing the security of households. There is the threat of state eradication programmes, violence and predation from rebel

> **Box 4.3: A coca memory**
>
> Sandra was among the women in coca-growing areas of Colombia interviewed by Isabel Pereira and Lucía Ramírez for the 2020 edited collection, *The Impact of Global Drug Policy and Women* (Box 4.1). She told them:
>
>> My first memory of coca is when my dad, seeing our desperate economic situation, decided to sell a cow and buy coca seeds to plant. After he sold his first harvest and came home [*Sandra smiles*] ... he left home with a little bag and came home with a huge sack – he brought us all kinds of things! And the next week, he said, "Okay, two of you are coming with me again to Puerto Asís to help with the shopping." He bought us shoes, boots, clothes, and he kept on doing it [over time]. So, my first memory of coca is one of happiness. It filled a big need.

groups and it frequently entails environmentally damaging impacts.

The OAS estimates that 2.5 million hectares of Amazonian forest were destroyed in Peru to grow coca, and over a million hectares of forest in Colombia, at a rate of four hectares cut for one hectare of coca planted. Anti-drug operations using crop burning, herbicide spraying and land clearance by private agribusinesses exacerbate this toll on the environment.

Supply control strategies in both military and development guise have not addressed the drivers or incentives for drug crop cultivation. At the same time, criminalization strategy has continued to generate added value and price stability for drug planting. As a result, two steps forward in supply reduction in one cultivation zone has simply led other territories and farmers to fill the market share, as demonstrated in the following snapshot, which summarizes the geographic shifts and stretch of supply zones for opium poppy.

Opium poppy cultivation: a snapshot

Progress in reducing opium poppy cultivation in the 'Golden Triangle' of Southeast Asian countries Thailand, Laos and Myanmar shifted the centre of gravity to the 'Golden Crescent' countries of Turkey, Pakistan and Iran in the 1960s and 1970s. Under intense US pressure, Turkey implemented an opium ban in 1971, moving to a state opium monopoly in 1974 and participation in the UN system of countries authorized to cultivate for global medical opiate quotas.

This did not contribute to a net global decline in illicit cultivation due to the resurgence of Myanmar, which by the mid-1990s was the source of over half of illicit global opium supply. This collapsed precipitously following the surrender of Shan state militia leader Khun Sa, the 'lord of opium', in 1996 but with the vacated illicit market share absorbed by Afghanistan.

There is a historical tradition of opium poppy cultivation in Afghanistan, but opium had played a minor role in the rural economy in comparison with neighbouring Iran and Pakistan. Export markets began to develop following the ban on opium poppy cultivation in Iran in 1955, which the US had robustly lobbied for.

Starting in the early 1980s and amid conflict between Soviet forces and the Islamicist mujahideen, Afghan opium poppy cultivation began a stellar three-decade climb, notwithstanding a brief collapse reported in 2001 following a ban on poppy planting imposed by the Taliban the previous year.

Afghan opium production in 1980 had been 200 metric tonnes (15 per cent of the global market). By 2002 it was over 3,500 metric tonnes, with cultivation spread across the country. US forces departing Afghanistan 20 years after invasion in 2002 left quadruple the area under opium poppy cultivation, and opium production of an estimated annual 5,000 metric tonnes. This was in the context of the US having spent $8.6 billion on counternarcotics programmes in Afghanistan between 2002 and 2017.

In the Americas, opium poppy farming in Mexico had been encouraged by the US to supply medical morphine during the US Civil War (1861–65). As the US moved towards tighter restrictions on opiates with the Harrison Narcotics Act of 1914, Mexico was pressured to terminate domestic cultivation and stop imports from China that were diverted to the Chinese diaspora in California.

The Mexican government enforced opium import restrictions in the mid-1920s. It catalysed an increase in domestic cultivation along well-established cross-border alcohol smuggling routes and consolidating the northwest of Mexico as the primary distribution point into North America through Ciudad Juárez in Chihuahua state.

Geographic proximity to the US allowed Mexican heroin suppliers to respond to supply shocks in opiate markets, for example caused by the interception of heroin trafficked from Myanmar, Turkey and Afghanistan. After the dismantling of the 'French Connection' heroin-trafficking route from Turkey through Marseille to the US East Coast, Mexican opium poppy quickly became the source of more than three quarters of the heroin in the US markets of the mid-1970s.

In the early 2000s, Colombia emerged as a significant opium poppy cultivating country, with the US DEA (Drug Enforcement Administration) estimating that over half of heroin available in the US was Colombian-sourced and supplied along the US East Coast. The Mexican market share fell back. Colombian poppy cultivation subsequently contracted towards the end of the decade with aggressive state eradication campaigns. This did not lead to a sustained fall in opium poppy volumes in the Andes. The decline in Colombia was offset by a reported doubling of Mexican poppy cultivation.

Coca geographies

As with patterns of opium poppy cultivation, illicit coca farming has been characterized by relocation between and within states, but geographically confined to Bolivia, Peru and Colombia. In the post-war period, illicit cocaine supply networks emerged later than opiates, with demand muted until the mid-1970s. Bolivia and Peru were early sources of illicit supply, with cultivation concentrated in the Chapare and Yungas regions of Bolivia, and the Huallaga Valley and Valley of the Apurímac, Ene and Mantaro rivers, also known as the VRAEM, in Peru. Illicit coca cultivation in Bolivia peaked in 1989 at 53,000 ha, with Peru registering a national high point of 115,300 ha in 1995.

Colombia had played a marginal role in coca cultivation but held a key position in cocaine hydrochloride processing and onward trafficking and distribution in the US. By 2001, the distribution of roles was revised, with Colombia responsible for three-quarters of the illicit coca farmed in the Andes. This followed a vertiginous increase in cultivation: in 1987, as US president Ronald Reagan was launching militarized anti-coca efforts in Bolivia, an estimated 26,000 ha was under coca cultivation. By 2001, 144,807 ha were reported, distributed across 22 of the 31 Colombian departments.

Mirroring trends in opium poppy, the increase in Colombia coca cultivation offset declines in Peru and Bolivia, which recorded a low of 20,000 ha. Illicit coca farming receded in Colombia in the 2000s and by 2012 the total area under coca cultivation was 48,000 ha, according to the UNODC. Thereafter Peru and Colombia resumed an upward trajectory as the area of Colombian cultivation tripled, culminating in the historic highs reported in the *2020 World Drug Report* and discussed in Chapter 1.

It is a dismal picture a century into international regulatory efforts and decades into a criminalization regime. Just as cultivation zones have reconfigured and relocated, so have the criminal groups engaged in transportation and trafficking out of source areas.

Around 90 per cent of profit in the cocaine trade is realized in the US. Just 1 per cent accrues to coca cultivators in the Andes, according to a 2013 study by the OAS. Nevertheless, policy makers have yet to devise a strategy that addresses the incentives for participation in supply activities that are created by criminalization for actors in either the Global North or countries of the Global South.

Box 4.4: The value of cocaine

In Colombian cocaine markets, analysis shows that an estimated 350 kg of coca leaves (costing approximately US$400) is required for the manufacture of 1 kg of first-stage cocaine.

The value of this 1 kg of cocaine is around US$800–$2,200 on export from Colombia, US$14,500 on arrival into the US, US$19,500 at mid-level wholesale and US$78,000 at retail level.

> Incorporating dilution and cutting with other substances into retail price assessment, *Economist* journalist Tom Wainwright in his 2016 book *Narconomics* calculated a retail price of US$122,000, representing a 30,000 per cent mark-up from the farm-gate coca leaf price.

The *2005 World Drug Report* estimates the value of illicit plant-based drugs in source countries at US$13 billion of a total retail value of US$322 billion.

While fractional, this revenue is an important source of jobs and livelihoods. In terms of the overall trade, the revenue share is so minor that eradication exercises must be on a massive, sustainable and worldwide scale to have any impact on prices in consumer countries.

Source-focused strategies targeting cultivators as a means of disabling and containing a billion-dollar global trade are 'A bit like trying to drive up the price of art by raising the price of paint. Gerhard Richter, whose canvases sell for up to $46 million, would not lose sleep if the price of the oil paints used in his works of art doubled, or even quintupled', according to Tom Wainwright. The logic of the international drug control is to step up seizures of paint.

From kingpins to cockroaches

Ronald Reagan's drug war offensive of the 1980s had many fronts. While intensifying efforts to eliminate the cultivation of drug plants, strategy also took on the kingpins – the cartel leaders, mafia bosses and paramilitary warlords running drug supply and distribution chains.

The criminal entrepreneurs who first capitalized on toughened post-war controls on heroin and subsequently cocaine ran simple operations. These were led by hierarchically structured, disciplined organizations with unbreakable bonds forged by family, place of birth, or some other form of fierce group loyalty.

The Sicilian mafia moved into the vacuum of heroin supply in US markets in the 1950s, sourcing product from Turkey, and South Asian suppliers operating out of Hong Kong. Marseille in France was an important hub for morphine refining, heroin manufacture and transhipment to New York, all operations running through Mafia-controlled ports and docks. Mexican cannabis cartels, and Colombian cocaine cartels operating on similar end-to-end supply principles, followed in the 1960s and 1970s. These organizations controlled all aspects of distribution, from the farm to the factory to American neighbourhoods.

In retrospect, we knew where we were with mafias and cartels. They logically corrupted easily corruptible state actors and political systems to ensure smooth export and import operations, they kept violence to a minimum to prevent unwarranted attention, and they poured significant sums of illicit money into communities and towns abandoned by central governments. This was a transactional and rarely a benevolent investment, intended to ensure authority, protection and social legitimacy. The old cartels usually concentrated their expertise on a specific plant-based drug and quietly blurred the lines between legal and illegal, licit and illicit economic activities, assisted by accountants, estate agents and bank managers responsible for laundering drug money and cleaning identities.

Contrast that with today's digitally connected 'disorganized' suppliers of benzos, amphetamine, ketamine and cocaine, operating through the postal system and social media platforms such as Telegram, SnapChat, Facebook and WhatsApp and promising delivery to your door to the hour. Behind these retailers is a myriad of small, transnational and violent trafficking and wholesale networks.

Europol estimated that around 5,600 organized crime groups were operating in Europe (in 2017), of which 30 to 40 per cent had loose network structures and 20 per cent had existed for only a short time. Compared with the operators of the 1970s, actors in this enterprise model are chaotic, unstable and unstructured.

So, what happened in the period in between? How did we go from international drug supply and distribution run through large hierarchical organizations to a contemporary proliferation of predatory gangs and criminal opportunists moving between a range of illicit and illegal economic activities?

The Hydra syndrome

US-led (or coerced) enforcement operations to take down drug kingpins were premised on the idea that

THE PROBLEM OF ENDLESS SUPPLY

decapitating the leadership of hierarchically structured trafficking groups would collapse cartel and mafia organizations and staunch drug supply. As with many of the assumptions that underpin criminalization strategy, this proved not to be the case.

For example, in Colombia over 300 smaller drug trafficking organizations moved into the vacuum left by the dismantling of the two major cartels in Colombia's cocaine trade. Juan Carlos Garzón and Ana María Rueda refer to the *efecto cucaracha* (cockroach effect) of crime actors scuttling to a safe place to recuperate and relaunch. Kingpin capture spawned 'criminal diasporas' scattered across countries and continents and looking for new opportunities in the illicit market.

Criminal entrepreneurs in Mexico were beneficiaries of the 'takedown' of Pablo Escobar of the Medellín cartel in 1993 and the leadership of the rival Cali cartel in 1996. Mexican organizations such as the Tijuana and Gulf cartels quickly consolidated control of cocaine transit and distribution routes from Colombia to the US.

Successful law enforcement operations to capture the heads of these two groups in turn created a vacuum for control of lucrative cocaine traffic that others quickly stepped into. This process of crime group diffusion and recycling, a negative outcome of kingpin strategies is referred to as 'the Hydra syndrome'. Like the serpent in Greek mythology that spawned two new heads when decapitated by Heracles, crime groups multiplied when leadership was removed.

Alfred McCoy, a much-respected historian of the opium trade, observed in 2019 that it is possible to capture drug lords, but not the sources of their power and wealth. Kingpins are 'expendable', while drug production and supply chains are 'mutable or moveable'.

From cartels to gangs: the prison industry

Colombian and Mexican crime groups pivoted cocaine trafficking eastwards to Europe as US counternarcotics cooperation with Andean countries intensified in the 1990s and 2000s. Caribbean states and West African countries were impacted by this diffusion and rerouting.

Jamaica's homicide rate peaked in 2009 at 62 per 100,000, according to the 2013 *World Drug Report*, as gangs such as the Shower Posse fought to control distribution into the US and the UK. More than seventy people were killed in a 2010 operation to arrest 'kingpin' Shower Posse leader Christopher Coke after a US extradition warrant in 2009.

In the Americas, the mafia and cartels have been replaced by the complex networked threat of transnational prison-based criminal gangs or *Maras*. Gang membership in Central America has been swollen by deportation processes from the US that have overwhelmingly focused on young men. Between 1997 and 2015, nearly a quarter of a million people were removed from the US to El Salvador. A third of them had a criminal conviction. More than 2.5 million people were deported by the Obama administration, principally determined by their gang membership and associated crimes.

There has been an increase in asylum claims by nationals from the Central American countries that Washington has deported hundreds of thousands of young men to. In 2005, nearly 4,000 applied for asylum in the US due to threats of gang-related violence. This increased to 26,000 a decade later (according to UNHCR, the UN Refugee Agency).

The growth of gangs and gang-related violence in Central and Latin America countries such as Brazil, El Salvador and Ecuador has been spurred by 'iron fist' (*mano duro*) government strategies. Gang membership and gang authority has spiralled in prisons overcrowded with men rounded up in anti-gang crackdowns and drug enforcement exercises.

It has been from within the region's prisons that gangs have become key actors in the cocaine trade and the movement of drugs and weapons, not just within their local towns or cities, but across countries and continents. A prime example is Brazil's Primeiro Comando da Capital (PCC; Capital's First Command), originally formed in 1993 to fight for prisoners' rights in the wake of the Carandiru Prison riot in São Paulo, according to a 2024 Insight Crime report. Through navigation of rival gang conflicts, cultivation of police and political ties, violence, and entrepreneurial skill, by 2023, the PCC had around 40,000 members, and a further 60,000 contractors involved in franchised operations, including in West Africa and Europe.

In country contexts as diverse as Australia, Indonesia, Spain, Sweden, Jamaica and South Africa, the geographical diffusion of trafficking networks has created violence linked to conflicts over local drug markets. Bereft of the 'old school' kingpins and *capos*, and traditions of operating quietly, contemporary drug gangs and crime organizations are wildly violent, noisy and competitive. There is no cultivation of the state, its infrastructure and agencies to ensure security of a single commodity export. Actors move between different profit opportunities, alliances and protection rackets. Gun- and people-trafficking and economic crimes (money laundering, kidnapping) can be far more lucrative and less risky than shifting drugs.

As discussed in Chapter 3, lockdown transformed the types of drugs that people wanted to consume. In the cocaine trade, it had the effect of accelerating trends of supply chain diffusion and diversification of wholesalers and exporters. Cocaine was not a popular substance during a period of zero recreational or public life. Border closures and restrictions on air travel were initially major obstacles to the transit of cocaine to markets in the US and Western Europe.

Mexican and Colombian crime groups controlling cocaine production and export out of Latin America responded to these altered conditions by shifting supply chains to the sea, and freight shipping, and submersible and semi-submersible craft dubbed 'narcosubs'. Only an estimated 2 per cent of global cargos are searched, making this a slow, if low-risk, means of moving cocaine product. Gangs, crime groups and corrupt officials with links to ports and dock facilities in countries such as Brazil and Ecuador were now favoured with cocaine franchises and distribution rights. On the receiving end of cocaine exports, new transnational connections and transactions forged between crime groups and criminal entrepreneurs in Latin America and Europe were reflected in the record cocaine seizures in places like Antwerp discussed at the beginning of this book.

Like other aspects of supply control strategy, the kingpin approach has not been successful in containing the growth of actors and organizations involved in illicit drug supply. Law enforcement operations to remove crime group leadership have not crippled organizations, broken trafficking infrastructures or encouraged lower-level criminal entrepreneurs to quit drug market opportunities. The strategy also seems to have had the negative outcome of violence. There has been a sharp rise in gun-related homicides linked to competition for drug-market share and broken agreements between ever-multiplying numbers of groups.

A modern old crisis

International drug control has failed to deter opium poppy, coca and cannabis cultivation over the century of control efforts. In the contemporary period, and with the cultivation problem still unresolved, technological innovation is driving more efficient cultivation and manufacturing processes.

Strain breeding is improving cultivation levels and yields, and new technologies make it possible for cultivators to bypass growing cycles and climatic obstacles such as limited water supply and low-quality soil.

In Afghanistan, the area under opium poppy cultivation in Helmand in 2012 was 157,000 hectares. By 2019, it was 344,000 hectares, expanding into arid desert using an estimated 67,000 solar arrays and water pumps available in local markets for US$5,000, according to fieldwork by David Mansfield.

In coca cultivation, protracted and labour-intensive processes such as drying and manually cutting coca leaves are increasingly replaced by gasoline-powered hedge-trimming machinery and oven-drying techniques. To 'wring' the cocaine alkaloid out of coca leaves, the traditional practice of stomping leaves (maceration) in pits of precursor chemicals and kerosene is being modernized: 'cartels have started using adapted washing machines as primitive centrifuges', Tom Wainwright writes in *Narconomics*. 'Sometimes these laboratories are installed in the backs of trucks that constantly trundle around the back roads of jungle, to avoid detection.'

International drug control is not positioned to counter dynamic change in drug plant cultivation *or* the growth of synthetic supply. There are no AD-type initiatives to address engagement with methamphetamine, MDMA or synthetic opiate manufacture activities as there are for drug plant cultivators, and at the same time, AD initiatives in drug crop cultivation zones are having the unintended consequence of encouraging synthetic drug market development.

THE PROBLEM OF ENDLESS SUPPLY

In Myanmar, the United Wa State Army accepted UN support for opium eradication after the government in Yangon announced a 15-year programme for eradication of all narcotics in 1999. They promptly shifted assets into methamphetamine manufacture. By 2002, an estimated 800 million tablets were manufactured annually and trafficked to Thailand, where 'synthetics supplanted opiates for most of Thailand's 2.5 million drug users, thereby fostering mass amphetamines use far more serious than the limited heroin addiction of earlier years' (according to Alfred McCoy, writing in 2019).

It seems that international drug control is fighting a battle that can never be won, either on the supply or the demand side. Two steps forward always result in three steps back, and usually other unintended harms. Decades of criminalization policy failure – clear and evident in the UNODC data – means that there is pressure for policy adjustment. In recent years some jurisdictions have unilaterally steered away from the prohibitive ethos of the treaties, for example by decriminalizing cannabis markets. However, as discussed in the following final chapter, the international system of drug policy governance imposes major constraints on paradigm shifts and policy change.

5
WHAT CHANCE OF DRUG POLICY REFORM?

If you hope for a world of justice and freedom, or even just evidence-based drugs policy, you have probably reached this final chapter somewhat depressed with drug policy and the drug situation. With good reason. We face the challenge of revolutionary synthetic drugs, new digital technologies, cheap cocaine and home-grown cannabis with a policy approach and strategic assumptions rooted in the norms, prejudices and pseudo-science of a century ago.

Conversely, if you are of the persuasion that criminalization fails because it is not enforced robustly, a reminder of the COVID-19 lockdown experience, in which illicit drug markets thrived when the world was closed and our movements were the most tightly policed and restricted. The arbitrary detentions, overcrowded prisons, executions and the burning of farmers' fields – all indications that enforcement is anything but lax – have not succeeded in reducing the supply or use of illicit drugs.

There is an accumulation of evidence that criminalization has been counterproductive for ambitions of a world free from the harms of narcotic substances. Strategy and enforcement are also wildly out of kilter with best practice approaches in policy processes and human rights obligations, as discussed in Chapter 2. Drug policy is not fit for contemporary purpose. Our problem is that the 'system' is incapable of change.

The international regime is resistant by design. Drug control institutions such as the Commission on Narcotic Drugs (CND), the International Narcotics Control Board (INCB) and the United Nations Office on Drugs and Crime (UNODC) have no mandate for revision or reform of strategy. They do not engage with evaluation, consultation or amendment processes that normally set failing policies on the road to revision or termination. They have a single purpose: to oversee compliance with the UN treaties.

The intergovernmental model of drug control that has evolved over the past century has been engineered to maintain the fragile consensus between states. Drug control resolutions and statements are carefully crafted, with months of tortuous negotiation over definitions and wording. Contentious terms and issues such as harm reduction have historically been swerved to avoid paralyzing dispute.

Most countries are also resistant to steps that might unravel the status quo. In a 2003 article, Cindy Fazey points to 'a surprising set of allies', including Sweden, Japan, Russia, Arab states and the US that strongly oppose change to the international criminalization framework. Not only is there opposition to any revisiting of fundamentals, but there is also no realistic alternative on the table – at least not a proposal that all states will get behind. And no state can go it alone. Minimizing the national level harms experienced in a global drug economy requires international collaboration and cross-border partnerships.

The 2000s did bring some optimism that the criminalization paradigm can be reformed from within, and that the UN treaties provide sufficient latitude to accommodate national initiatives and decisions on reform. There has been a snowballing of local decriminalization initiatives, mainly involving cannabis. This movement away from criminalization has been led by national governments and regional and municipal authorities around the world, including a raft of US states and Australian territories.

Reform initiatives are welcome and urgent but, as discussed next, the benefits are neutered. The change processes that you may be familiar with such as medical cannabis prescription have to work within the international criminalization paradigm. Reform jurisdictions have explicitly delimited the scope of drug policy revision to maintain their wider responsibilities under the international drug treaties. Drug policy changes have been explicit in marrying limited local consumer reforms with harsher responses to trafficking and illicit supply offences. Decriminalization initiatives consequently risk embedding existing injustices in the policing of everyday drug-related activities.

Public crisis and the roots of local reform

In the 1980s, the US led efforts to toughen up enforcement of the criminalization regime. As discussed in the previous chapter, the Reagan presidency (1981–89) militarized US supply-control efforts in the cocaine-producing countries of South America. On the domestic front there was a slew of draconian legal initiatives, including the Sentencing Reform Act (1984), eliminating parole for most federal prisoners; the Comprehensive Crime Control Act (1984), which enshrined 'civil forfeiture' into law; the Anti-Drug Abuse Act (1986), which increased mandatory minimum sentences for drug offences; Executive Order 12564 (1986), establishing random drug testing for federal employees, and the Drug Abuse Act (1988), which introduced the death penalty for drug 'kingpins'.

The punitive turn was replicated in other countries aligned with the US. Governments in Western Europe and Australia leveraged tougher drug laws to counter the increase in heroin and synthetic drug use. As in the 1960s and 1970s, more coercive enforcement responses in the 1980s were also a useful tool for policing youth dissent and anti-government mobilization such as raves and other protests of the neoliberal era.

The adoption of a 'zero tolerance' path, as encouraged by the 1988 United Nations Convention Against Illicit Traffic in Narcotic Drugs and Psychotropic Substances, was exemplified in paraphernalia laws prohibiting the possession of crack pipes, bongs and injecting syringes. It was at this point in regime evolution that international drug control had to address an epidemic of disease that was linked to injection with dirty, unsterilized needles.

When HIV/AIDS crossed into the community of People Who Inject Drugs (PWID) in the capitalist West, Soviet East and China in the early 1980s, UN drug control institutions, the drug treaties and national criminalization laws were an obstacle to urgent and necessary interventions to prevent disease spread.

Harm reductionists in European cities such as Liverpool, Amsterdam, Zurich and Frankfurt urged government interventions that lessened the dangers of injecting drug use. This included the provision of clean injecting equipment to PWID. Harm reduction philosophy takes a pragmatic, non-judgmental and humanistic position, accepting the inevitability that people will engage in risky behaviours. The priority is reducing associated dangers to health. In the 1980s, the single focus was HIV and other blood-borne virus risks (Hepatitis B) among injectors.

Just as condoms prevented the spread of HIV/AIDS through sexual activity, getting sterile injecting equipment to injectors was the most effective way of preventing the spread of HIV/AIDS linked to injecting behaviours. In countries such as Portugal, where 60 per cent of injectors were HIV positive, and Switzerland, which had an estimated 10,000 injecting drug users and the highest rate of HIV infection in Western

Europe in the mid-1980s, political authorities quickly realized that harm reduction interventions would be ineffective if stigmatized and isolated PWID did not come forward to pick up sterile but criminalized drug paraphernalia. Laws and attitudes had to change if HIV was to be controlled and prevented. The experience of 'shock events' such as HIV epidemics and public health crises led Switzerland, Portugal and several other jurisdictions down the path of decriminalization.

Decriminalization in practice

The 2010s saw a significant number of drug policy reform initiatives. Legal and regulatory changes in jurisdictions across the world variously decriminalized the possession and use of medical cannabis, recreational cannabis, and personal-use cannabis cultivation. A handful of countries (Uruguay, Canada, Malta, Luxembourg, Germany) and many individual US states have gone a step further and introduced regulated adult recreational cannabis markets ('legalization'), and ending the status of cannabis as a 'narcotic'.

Some countries, including Spain (1983), the Czech Republic (1990), Portugal (2001), Chile (2005), Mexico (2009) and Switzerland (2013), have gone further, decriminalizing the possession of all controlled drugs for personal use.

In contexts such as North America and Australia, where federal governments have been reluctant to introduce reforms, states and provinces have been the motor of change. For example, Australian Capital

Territory became the first Australian jurisdiction to decriminalize possession of (nine) drugs in small quantities. British Columbia province in Canada decriminalized possession of 2.5 grams of opioids, cocaine, methamphetamine and MDMA, effective from January 2023.

The path of decriminalization has commonly started with regulations or legal changes to allow harm reduction measures such as sterile injecting provision and (oral) opioid substitution medicines, evolving to more contentious interventions such as safe injecting facilities with supervised care pioneered by organizations such as Insite in Vancouver, Canada. Insite was opened in 2003, in response to a sharp increase in both HIV infection, reaching an annual incidence of 19 per cent among PWID, and fatal overdoses.

Drug decriminalization has typically been the next step, intended to destigmatize drug use and people who use drugs, and to put drug strategy on a public health footing. The term 'decriminalization' is something of a misnomer. Most of these initiatives are police diversion or depenalization schemes: possession remains an offence and police continue to enforce the law, but with infractions dealt with through civil, not criminal, proceedings.

The process of decriminalization can be *de jure*, with policy reform enshrined in law through statute or constitutional court decision. Examples of *de jure* decriminalization of cannabis for personal use include South Australia (1987), Australian Capital Territory

(1992), Northern Territory (1996), Jamaica (2015), Belize (2017), Thailand (2018), Antigua and Barbuda (2018) and Ghana (2020). Less frequently change is *de facto*. In this approach, the law does not change but enforcement practices do. An example of this model is the Netherlands, where prosecutorial guidelines dating from 1976 do not require the law to be enforced for personal use possession of cannabis or cultivation of up to five cannabis plants.

Threshold quantities are an important element of decriminalization schemes. This refers to the amount of a particular substance that an individual is allowed to be in possession of (or to cultivate) without being subject to criminal penalties. Threshold quantities can be contentious, and determine the acceptability of schemes to policy stakeholders including the police, the medical community and people who use drugs. Too high, and decriminalization is challenged as too liberal. Too low – below typical user levels – and policing and arrests will likely continue unchanged.

Threshold quantities can be binding and strictly applied, with the individual risking more serious charges of trafficking and distribution if they are minutely over the threshold. Indicative threshold quantities allow law enforcement discretion if the individual is over the threshold but not suspected of involvement in supply. In some decriminalization models, no threshold is set, and it is for the individual to demonstrate to law enforcement or criminal justice authorities that the amount in their possession is intended for personal use only.

Table 5.1: Comparative threshold quantities for personal use possession

	Cannabis herb	Cocaine	MDMA	Heroin
Spain	100 g	7.5 g	2.4 g	3 g
Portugal	25 g	2 g	1 g	1 g
Czech Republic	15 g	1 g	1.2 g	1.5 g
Mexico	5 g	0.5 g	40 mg	50 mg

Regulated supply and cannabis clubs

A challenge for decriminalization strategies relates to supply. Policy reforms that liberalize but do not provide access to cannabis can strengthen the illicit trade. Acknowledging this risk, most decriminalizing jurisdictions have depenalized cannabis cultivation for personal use with thresholds. For example, a maximum of five home cannabis plants are permitted in Jamaica, four in Antigua and Barbuda, and two in Australian Northern and Capital Territories. In the US, the range is from twenty-five plants, in Alaska, to a typical six, as in California.

By 2020 social club models that allowed licensed collective cannabis cultivation and harvest sharing between groups of between five and forty-five registered adults had been introduced in the Czech Republic, Costa Rica, Chile, Italy, Jamaica, Malta, Mexico, Switzerland, Uruguay, and the US states of Oregon, Nevada, Maine, Colorado and Alaska (as reported by Tom Decorte and Mafalda Pardal).

By contrast with decriminalization, some countries have removed all criminal penalties relating to cannabis, formalizing cannabis once again as a legal consumer good. Uruguay was the first country to regulate every level of the cannabis market, in line with President José Mujica's 2012 Strategy for Life and Co-Existence. Succinctly explaining why, Mujica set out: 'someone has to be the first'. Canada followed in 2018.

As with other intoxicants such as alcohol or tobacco, cannabis regulation determines who can purchase cannabis (age, residency), in what form (edibles, buds), strength, price, in what type of location (pharmacies, licensed commercial shops, cannabis clubs), at what times (similar to pub opening hours) and where cannabis can and cannot be consumed, all overseen by a new regulatory authority.

In Uruguay, citizens and permanent residents over the age of 18 who registered with the new Institute for Regulation and Control of Cannabis (IRCCA) were permitted to purchase up to 10 g per week from licensed pharmacies, grow up to six female flowering cannabis plants per household for own consumption (to a maximum 480 g annual production) or form a cannabis club of between 15 and 45 members. Each club is permitted to cultivate up to 99 plants per year but not dispense more than 480 g to each club member. Surplus yield must be submitted to the IRCCA.

Legalization is acknowledged to contravene the UN drug treaties, which expressly prohibit recreational use. Reform states maintain that regulation is influenced by public health considerations and therefore within the spirit of the treaties.

Conditions for change – and lack of it

A British reader may be surprised to learn of these developments in other parts of the world. The UK has been in suspended animation for decades, tied to drug laws from the 1970s. While fellow G7 and Commonwealth countries reoriented drug strategies towards improved health and social justice outcomes, the succession of seven Conservative Party Home Office ministers between 2010 and 2022 aimed to strengthen the punishment and deterrence framework of the 1971 Misuse of Drugs Act.

This leaning into traditional strategies of repression and coercion was despite a crisis of record drug use, treatment services that a government-commissioned review by Dame Carol Black (2020) found to be unfit for purpose, and record drug-related deaths. As discussed earlier, there were 4,859 drug-related overdose fatalities recorded by the Office for National Statistics in England and Wales in 2021, the highest number since records began in 1993.

The Conservative government's ten-year drug strategy published in 2021 raised experts' and service providers' concerns because of 'unevidenced and harmful measures to deter drug use by means of punishment' and the 'continuation of policies rooted in enforcement' (according to Holland and colleagues in 2023). A 2022 government consultation paper, 'Swift, Certain, Tough: New Consequences for Drug Possession', proposed removing the passports and driving licences of people convicted for drug possession offences.

WHAT CHANCE OF DRUG POLICY REFORM?

At an October 2022 conference, Conservative police commissioners (locally elected police oversight boards) called for cannabis to be reclassified from a Class B to a Class A drug and in 2023, plans to schedule nitrous oxide (laughing gas) were announced, a decision that went against the expert advice of the government's Advisory Council on the Misuse of Drugs (ACMD).

The recommendations of the ACMD expert body have been routinely ignored by Conservative governments, and by Labour before that (as discussed in Chapter 2, the Labour government sacked its chief drug adviser, Professor David Nutt, in 2009). For three years, the Conservative government denied a Freedom of Information request to release a 2016 ACMD report detailing the negative impacts of criminalization in the UK and advising decriminalization (Busby 2023).

Despite having among the highest per capita rates of drug use and drug-related deaths, and a significant lobby for drug policy change, bipartisan agreement on criminalization prevails between the country's two main political parties, even if senior figures tended to endorse drug policy reform before or after they left office. Consider, for example, the quotes in Box 5.1 from former prime minister Boris Johnson.

The prescription of cannabis-based medications was permitted in the UK in cases of 'exceptional clinical need' in 2018, but as of 2024, only a handful of patients had NHS prescriptions. Patients for whom cannabis-based oils and medications were a positive clinical option, including children with rare forms of

> **Box 5.1: Double standards and doublespeak**
>
> I think there is a risk governments are out of touch [...] I have some perfectly respectable neighbours, good bourgeois types [...] they roll up a spliff and smoke it together, and yet they are in breach of the law. (Boris Johnson, 2000)
>
> We are going to look at new ways of penalising them. Things that will actually interfere with their lives so we will look at taking away passports and driving licences. (Boris Johnson, 2020)

epilepsy, were forced to rely on private prescriptions that were costly (£2,000 per month) and poorly understood by police.

The chair of the All-Party Parliamentary Group on Medical Cannabis under Prescription, Tonia Antoniazzi, argued:

> In any circumstance, this is a severe financial burden for families already having to cope with very sick children [...] the families to which we refer simply do not have time [...] They are emotionally and financially broken and their children are at risk of being without their life-transforming medicine within weeks.

At the same time, and as outlined in a 2023 House of Commons report, the UK is the world's biggest producer and exporter of legal cannabis for medical and scientific purposes, producing 329 metric tonnes in 2021.

Constitutional arrangements have also been an obstacle to drug policy revisions in the UK. Safe injecting rooms were a flashpoint of contention between the UK Parliament in Westminster and the Scottish Government in Edinburgh. Protracted opposition from Westminster disregarded a solid record of reducing overdose deaths and disease in contexts such as Vancouver, Copenhagen, Switzerland and Germany. The Thistle safer drug consumption facility finally opened in Glasgow in January 2025.

The drug policy situation in the UK and the retention of regressive strategy despite serious policy failings begs the question, how do some countries get to the liberal end of the drug policy spectrum, while others pivot to excessive violence and 'drug wars' or, like the UK and some Scandinavian countries, just stand still?

As discussed earlier, crisis situations have been an important incentive for authorities to begin the arduous path of shifting strategy, process and norms. But other institutional mechanisms and facets of social and political culture are necessary for reform. Some of these are highlighted next.

Political leadership is a fundamental condition of drug policy change (a severe problem in British drug policy). Without high-level political support championing change agendas, reform initiatives are easily marginalized and discredited.

Support for decriminalization from law enforcement, the medical community and religious leaders is another important condition of policy change. When police and clinicians come to the view that criminalization strategies are unworkable and counterproductive, this creates momentum for political leaders, the media and public to engage with decriminalization debates. Conversely, hostility from these influential policy stakeholders can derail reform initiatives.

In terms of the mechanics of policy change, this has varied across reform jurisdictions and includes popular referenda on decriminalization (US states, Switzerland) and constitutional and legal appeal processes (Argentina in 2009, Colombia in 1994 and South Africa in 2018). In these cases, litigants have successfully argued that the UN treaties violate rights and obligations set out in national constitutions.

Electoral systems, and the extent to which these facilitate or discourage single-issue drug policy reform parties, or conversely, populist anti-drug movements are another factor influencing reform trajectories.

Government expert commissions, convened in places such as Jamaica, Portugal, Ghana, Switzerland and Malta, have been another important tool to shift repressive criminalization laws, bringing together different stakeholders to pluralize policy input, assess data and evidence, and develop alternative approaches.

The presence of a responsible media publicizing unacceptable policy outcomes, and journalistic reporting that steers public perceptions away from stigmatizing stereotypes (see, for example, the work of

Travis Lupick, Mattha Busby, and J.S. Rafaeli and Max Daly at *Vice* magazine) are also factors in successful policy revision processes. Britain struggles on many of these fronts.

Some jurisdictions have a positive public sentiment that allows more liberal laws to motor forward. It is something that runs deeper than other important elements of the policy change story, like shifts in public opinion towards drugs. It permeates the political culture and is shared by countries that have in the past lived under authoritarian regimes. For example, in Spain, Portugal, the Czech Republic and South Africa, criminalization is associated with intrusive state surveillance and police harassment. Drug decriminalization in this context is a means of (re-)establishing individual rights and freedoms.

Small steps and cascade effects: shifts in international drug control

At the beginning of this book, it was argued that nation states are circumscribed in the development of national strategies for managing psychoactive substances. Countries are tied into UN treaty obligations and party to an international drug control regime that is designed to maintain the drug criminalization consensus. As detailed in earlier chapters, the US has been a pivotal actor in the design, construction and universalization of the treaty framework and used coercive measures such as sanctions to force country compliance and collaboration with the international system. How then have the national-level decriminalization initiatives outlined over previous pages been possible?

There are four interlinked explanations. Firstly, as discussed earlier in this chapter, the decriminalization initiatives are overwhelmingly limited to cannabis and to consumption. Bolivia is the only country to have addressed supply-side aspects, other than for cannabis, with the introduction of regulated coca markets during the presidency of Evo Morales (2006–19). The move was successful in reducing illicit coca farming but faced strong resistance from international drug control institutions and from the US.

In all other aspects, reform jurisdictions continue to respect the content and the steer of the UN drug treaties. In this respect they are small-c 'conservative' changes that work within the international criminalization paradigm and conciliatory to domestic opponents of policy change. This includes through tough enforcement action against illicit cannabis markets.

A second reason why these international decriminalization initiatives have been able to thrive is the changing position of the US federal government.

The US: from prohibition proselytizing to regime liberalizing

The US has had a preponderant influence over international drug control so we should expect that any shift in the sands of US drug policy will have reverberations on the international stage and cascade effects in other countries. This has indeed been the case.

WHAT CHANCE OF DRUG POLICY REFORM?

The use in US states of ballot initiatives to allow medical cannabis, starting in California in 1996, created a major headache for the federal government in Washington. Under federal law, cannabis remains a Schedule 1 most dangerous drug. Nevertheless, authorized access to medical cannabis snowballed at state level, including through popular ballots in Oregon, Alaska and Washington (1998); Maine (1999); Nevada and Colorado (2000); Montana (2004); Michigan (2008) and Arizona (2010). In Hawaii, regulated medical cannabis was introduced by the state legislature (2000), a route that was followed by other states, including Vermont (2004), Rhode Island (2006), New Mexico (2007), New Jersey (2010), Delaware (2011) and Connecticut (2012).

The Barack Obama presidency (2009–17) did not respond aggressively to the unravelling of federal drug law authority, even as this accelerated in 2012 with ballots in Colorado and Washington state supporting adult recreational cannabis markets. A decade later, medical cannabis was legal in 39 of the 50 US states. Adult regulated cannabis markets – a direct contravention of the 1961 UN Single Convention – were operating in 24 of these.

How to accommodate the autonomy of US states in cannabis policy while simultaneously leading the world in a war on drugs? The US federal government responded with the so-called Brownfield Doctrine of 2014. Obama's Assistant Secretary of State for International Narcotics and Law Enforcement William Brownfield outlined a new approach of flexible interpretation of the UN drug treaties and toleration of different national drug strategies. For Brownfield, what unified countries in this new era of drug market change was the commitment to work collaboratively to prevent illicit supply. In sum, 'all agree to combat and resist the criminal organizations – not those who buy, consume, but those who market and traffic the product for economic gain'.

With the threat of US sanctions, interventions or decertification removed, other jurisdictions were more confident taking national decriminalization initiatives forward, despite the criticism from UN drug control bodies such as the INCB.

International regime adjustment: a thousand flowers bloom

The pace of change is glacial within the international drug-control regime. Recent small shifts within the authority of bodies such as the 53-country CND have nevertheless been achieved. This is a third explanation for the favourable drug reform environment: a modest space for change that was opened up by the more liberal position of the US government. Gentle institutional and governance reforms at UN level have also been necessary to reset the international policy consensus amid demands from a growing number of countries for public health-led approaches and scientifically informed drug scheduling.

Adjustment is contentious but has been possible. For example, in 2021 the removal of cannabis from Schedule IV of the 1961 UN Single Convention (most dangerous and no medical benefits) passed with a majority of just two country votes.

In a system that has diverted pressure for change for decades, the impact of relatively minor shifts is sizeable. Ending the Schedule IV status of cannabis has widened the regulatory space for licensing, medical research and therapeutic access, including in the treatment of chronic conditions such as Parkinson's and Alzheimer's disease, multiple sclerosis and arthritis, for pain management in cancer and HIV, and in the treatment of neurologic illnesses such as depression, anxiety, anorexia and epilepsy.

As an example of the pharmaceutical and commercial dynamics pressuring change, cannabis medications developed by British biomedical companies for the treatment of epilepsy (Epidyolex) and multiple sclerosis (Sativex) had net worldwide product sales in 2021 of US$658.3 million and US$18.5 million, respectively. This is in the context of cannabis remaining a Schedule I narcotic in the UN drug treaties.

The increase in demand for cannabis plant materials for pharmaceutical extraction of (non-psychoactive) CBD and THC has created new commercial opportunities in cannabis cultivation. States are adapting national drug laws accordingly. Lesotho was the first country in Africa to grant administrative licences for cannabis and hemp farming in 2017. Zimbabwe, South Africa, Malawi, eSwatini, Uganda, Zambia and Rwanda followed. In the Caribbean, regulated commercial cultivation for medical CBD/THC extraction in Jamaica, Barbados, and Antigua and Barbuda was expected to generate revenues of up to US$650 million in licensing and export sales by 2025, according to *The Economist* in 2019.

In the Albanian model of commercial cultivation announced in 2022, companies tendering for the first round of 15-year cultivation licences were required to have capital of €8 million, five to ten hectares of privately owned land (up to 150 hectares for hemp), and a minimum of 15 employees. The move intended to incorporate Albania into a lucrative Balkans pharmaceutical cannabis sector that was thriving with major investment from Canadian firms. For example, Canadian-based International Cannabis Corp (ICC) had licences for cannabis cultivation, and for the production, distribution, storage and export of cannabis, cannabis derivatives and industrial hemp in Macedonia, Denmark, Poland, Greece, Portugal, Poland, Lesotho, South Africa and Colombia.

Minor scheduling modifications, the shifting position of the US federal government and efforts to pluralize drug policy processes have enabled international drug control to lumber forward into a more modern age. These small steps, and many of the local and national cannabis decriminalization initiatives, have been made possible because of the work of campaign groups. Coalitions of civil society actors have been the primary source of reform pressure on the US, on other national governments, and on the UN. Their activities are a fourth explanation for the raft of decriminalization and regulation initiatives globally.

Advocacy

NGO networks have pushed legal and constitutional challenges to drug laws and enforcement practices that violate human rights and health protections. As with the anti-opium agitation over a century ago, which was influential in steering the international community down the path of criminalization, so many national groups for policy change operate under international umbrellas, embracing global activism as the most effective way of countering the universal criminalization strategy.

Transnational activism spanning grassroots networks and high-level political lobbying expanded and professionalized in the 2000s. This was facilitated by processes of democratization, liberalization, and technological change. Communication and information sharing between different national organizations enabled the development of collaborative reform and campaign agendas.

Lobbies for drug policy change incorporate a diversity of actors, interests and organizational forms, including scientists, students, academics, politicians, law enforcement personnel and military veterans; people who use or have used or who cultivate drugs; and families that have experienced the negative outcomes of criminalization, such as overdose death and overincarceration of loved ones. As explained in the discussion on international and national drug policy processes, these voices and experiences are typically excluded in drug policy deliberations and evaluations.

> **Box 5.2: Happy, II**
>
> In my 2020 interview with Happy from INPUD, they told me how they had been supported by transnational networks:
>
> > I started working as a coordinator at the network and it was hard. We had nothing at that time, but there was this person from France and she was cool. She started teaching me many things and getting me in touch with different people. In the end, we made it. We got the first grant from UNESCO [United Nations Educational, Scientific and Cultural Organization] to educate in 12 schools about harm reduction and effects of drug use and maternity/childcare – things like that. It went well, and when it was finishing, we got another grant from OSIEA [Open Society Institute for East Africa] which was for two years. That's when I started being invited to different areas, getting to be known and getting to know other people.

Alliance-building between groups in intersecting policy areas that are impacted by criminalization has forged a broad coalition for reform of policy and strategy. For example, in contrast to the 1980s and 1990s, when development and human rights organizations fretted over reputational risk associated with working on drug policy, concerns have been overcome. The 'poison chalice' (so labelled by Duncan Green in 2020) has been grasped by several organizations such as CAFOD, OXFAM, Amnesty International and Human Rights Watch, which have produced a slew of reports on the negative impacts and the violence of criminalization. Importantly, the United Nations Development Programme (UNDP) and Office of the High Commissioner for Human Rights (OHCHR) adopted positions critical of criminalization during this period.

Think tanks, NGOs and elite-level advocacy have provided support to the drafting of decriminalization proposals, laws and regulations, and supported capacity building of policy makers and political parties around the world. The Global Commission on Drug Policy, established in 2011, is an example of this type of influential lobby. The Commission draws together former presidents of countries including Brazil, Switzerland, Chile, Colombia, Poland, South Africa, Nigeria, Mauritius and Mexico, prime ministers from Greece, Haiti, New Zealand and Timor Leste, and until his death in 2018, Kofi Annan, former UN Secretary General. Former UK deputy prime minister Nick Clegg is also a commissioner.

In 2011, the 'taboo-breaking' Report of the Global Commission called for a paradigm shift towards improved health and social justice outcomes, a message echoed in regional groupings such as the Latin American Commission on Drugs and Democracy, and the West Africa Commission on Drugs.

The drug policy reform movement chalked up a series of major successes in the 2010s and 2020s. To date, the liberalization and legalization initiatives that groups pressured for have delivered on many of the intended goals. However, despite some positive outcomes and impacts of decriminalization, the reform momentum faces major pushback.

Reform in context and contestation

Given the short duration of decriminalization and regulation initiatives, the number of evaluations available is small. Comparative assessment of different jurisdictions is difficult due to the diverging aims, objectives and priorities of reform processes and the type of drug that is the focus of the legal intervention. Nevertheless, positive results can be identified even if these are unevenly distributed across countries. A couple of key findings are presented here.

Firstly, decriminalizing drugs and regulating adult recreational cannabis use has not made these substances more attractive to younger people or to the wider population. In most reform jurisdictions there has been no discernible change in rates of drug use. This contrasts with non-reform countries such as the UK, Ireland and Nordic countries where user rates have maintained an upward trajectory.

To maximize the benefits of decriminalization, legal and regulatory changes to the status of cannabis (or any other drug) must be one part of a wider package of interventions to support crime-vulnerable communities and people who use drugs problematically. Decriminalization and legalization initiatives must also be accompanied by training and resources for professional bodies such as police and probation services, social workers and teachers. Public education campaigns are also important in supporting the implementation of new models and reducing the risk of potential harms, for example in relation to driving after legally smoking cannabis.

By reducing criminal penalties and prioritizing health improvements over stigmatizing norms, decriminalization is associated with an uptake of harm reduction and treatment services. Ameliorating the fear of arrest or harassment by law enforcement creates space for those with lived and living experience to take up services and participate in the design and delivery of interventions. Decriminalization alongside programmes to reduce illicit substance use harms, such as drug checking and the provision of sterile injecting equipment and crack-smoking pipes (to stop pipe sharing), correlate with a decrease in HIV and other infectious disease, overdoses and incidences of drug-related death.

Decriminalization can foster an environment supportive of multi-agency interventions that can better identify and support vulnerable individuals, reduce their exposure to drug-related harms, and which can begin addressing the complex of factors that underpin problematic use, for example, homelessness, trauma, partner violence and unmedicated other mental and physical health needs.

Decriminalization improves collaboration between police, drug users and service providers. New partnerships allow information such as new drug types in circulation, incidents of drug contamination and the location of vulnerable people to be shared. Early warning systems position health services, police and NGO networks to better anticipate and respond to emergencies such as bad batches of a particular drug, or the emergence of new, more potent or impure substances in different drug scenes.

The diversion of low-level, non-violent drug law offenders away from the criminal justice system alleviates pressure on police, prosecution and prison systems. Decriminalization allows law enforcement expertise and resources to refocus onto more complex high-level criminality and violence. The incentive for the police to target 'low hanging fruit' to boost arrest rates is removed. The adoption of new policing procedures that are seen to be fair improves the legitimacy of police services, the credibility of the law, and confidence in the criminal justice system.

Diversion away from prison for drug possession, low level cultivation and for non-violent offences linked to drug use (for example shoplifting) is associated with reduced rates of recidivism and family dislocation, and a fall in rates of property and acquisitive crime.

Other reported positive outcomes of cannabis decriminalization include reduced progression from cannabis to 'harder' drugs, and a decline in rates of polydrug use. Research in North America found a link between decriminalization of cannabis, lower levels of prescription opiate use, and reduced incidence of opiate-related hospitalization, overdose and dependence.

There is little evidence that decriminalization and legal regulation has led to the types of 'drug tourism' feared by critics, or an influx of problematic drug users from other municipalities, states or countries. Policy shift also generates income for public services, and investment and employment opportunities in local economies. In Canada, the first year of 'recreational' sales generated a CAN$153 million spend on non-medical cannabis products (according to CannStandard in 2022). By 2023, this had increased to CAN$5.2 billion led by flower, vape and edible products distributed through 800 regulated outlets.

The more things change, the more they stay the same: exclusion and inequality in reform initiatives

The speed and direction of some drug law changes has been criticized by reform advocates. For example, major inequities and injustices have emerged in newly regulated cannabis sectors in North America. The end of criminalization brought a flood of investment into commercial cannabis. As reported by *Forbes* magazine, in 2020, the 'Green Rush' saw large mega-cultivators with 'digitally smart, robotics-abetted facilities' and 'near science-fiction levels of sophistication' quickly dominate the retail market.

In the North American commercial cannabis model, and distinct from the not-for-profit cannabis clubs in contexts such as Uruguay and Malta, the so-called 'Big Marijuana' industry squeezed out community cultivators and retailers. Small marijuana entrepreneurs struggled with under-capitalization and lack of collateral to raise finance. Exclusive distribution agreements between cannabis supply and distribution outlets edged out minor players. Where previous cannabis-related criminal convictions have not been expunged, this is another entry barrier for small-scale entrepreneurs. There has been major change and no change at all in the move from criminalized to regulated markets. This situation sustains the illicit cannabis sector, and the vulnerability of these same entrepreneurs to old problems of police attention and criminal convictions.

In medical cannabis cultivating countries in Africa and the Balkans, the requirements for participation in the licensed cannabis cultivation sector are also onerous. Farmers without the necessary land and financial resources for large-scale commercial cultivation have been forced out of the Green Revolution, an opportunity lost in terms of potential poverty reduction and development gains.

Another significant setback for development relates to the situation of the traditional cannabis plant cultivating countries of the Global South such as Morocco, Lebanon and Mexico. After decades of repressive policies to suppress a now legal agricultural commodity (in some countries), farmers in historic cultivation zones cannot export to jurisdictions that have adult recreational cannabis markets. This would likely go against national laws on cultivation (criminalized in line with the 1961 UN Single Convention) and inter-state trafficking.

Experts such as Dave Bewley Taylor and Martin Jelsma argue that a complex bilateral process of *'inter se'* treaty modification is the only way around this situation under the current UN drug treaty regime. In laypersons' terms, this means an export and import agreement separately negotiated between, for example, Morocco and Canada. Big Marijuana in North America and large-scale private cannabis investors in Europe have little interest in pushing these untested flexibilities of the UN treaty system. This is another opportunity lost for those communities that have been most exposed to the violence and dislocation of criminalization.

There are other tensions within decriminalizing jurisdictions and debates. In the activist and user community, progress in advancing regulatory reform around cannabis and psychedelics has led to concerns that users of other types of drugs such as heroin and cocaine are being left behind, and movement solidarity undermined.

Drug policy adjustments that have been intentionally timid to contain policy 'spoilers' and other critics are ineffective. For example, low threshold quantities for drug possession maintains an intrusive role for police in drug policing and can increase the risk of arrest for being over the allowed volume.

Illicit markets continue to sit alongside legal cannabis markets when consumers are unhappy with the strength or the price of regulated products, or the types of social interaction that the purchase involves, for example, preferring to buy from an old friend rather than in a commercial shop.

Box 5.3: Psychedelic renaissance

Psychedelic and hallucinogenic substances such as MDMA, LSD, ayahuasca and psilocybin distort perceptions of reality, time, identity, colour, sound and touch in users (synaesthesia). The drugs are associated with a resetting and re-ordering of brain functioning.

Over 40,000 patients were prescribed LSD therapy (mainly in the US) in the 1950s and 1960s, usually one to three sessions with a dose of psychedelic medicine. After strict controls on LSD in the 1971 UN Convention on Psychotropic Substances, psychedelic therapy continued underground, with centres in Czechoslovakia, Canada and the US.

Groups campaigning for regulated use of psychedelic medicines include military veterans in the US and the UK. This has brought heightened visibility and political leverage. Substantial philanthropic funding supports clinical trials in treatment of post-traumatic stress disorder (PTSD) and chronic depression. This has been channelled through the Multidisciplinary Association for the Study of Psychedelics (MAPS). Over 300 psychedelics trials have been authorized in the US. Current MDMA and psilocybin trials show a 60–80 per cent success rate in PTSD treatment compared to 30–40 per cent for existing anti-depressant medications such as SSRIs. In 2019, the Phase 3 trials were granted Breakthrough Therapy Designation by the US Food and Drug Administration addressing 'urgent and life-threatening

> conditions in patients who do not currently have promising treatment options'.
>
> Criminalization is an obstacle to rapid roll-out of trials. The internet has opened up new avenues for self-help, including access to psychedelic drugs, therapists and organized 'cleansing' and healing ceremonies.

By relying on individual political leaders to champion reform, decriminalization and legalization initiatives are proving vulnerable to rollback and containment. Policy debate in many decriminalizing and legalizing jurisdictions is divisive, and modest reform steps have been polarizing and have galvanized conservative pushback.

Religious leaders, the abstinence lobby and conservative family associations have been prominent critics of policy change in contexts such as Malta, Canada and the US. The UN drug treaties legitimize resistance, moral – rather than scientific – drug policy debates, and the pressure to roll back decriminalization initiatives. Further underscoring the vulnerability of drug policy change, the second Donald Trump presidency reversed the liberal track of the Brownfield Doctrine. At the first CND meeting in Vienna attended by the new Trump team in March 2025, US delegates recycled arcane narrative, tropes and strategies that drew heavily on the rhetoric of, but not the lessons learned from, the violent and militarized Ronald Reagan years.

Reform jurisdictions have not seen a consolidation of the new norms and narratives that stress drugs as a health issue, not a policing matter. Decriminalization and legalization initiatives of the 2010s and 2020s have become a wedge issue in the context of nativist, xenophobic and nationalist campaigns against migration, immorality, and pernicious external influences. As such, this book has come full circle: we are back to the early 1900s.

So what *is* drug policy for?

Global public policy, and the arduous process of knitting together agreement between sovereign countries on a unified policy response, is typically associated with a public good, for example protection from disease, global poverty or climate crisis. These problems, and their impacts, cut across national boundaries. International collaboration and new forms of global governance are therefore required to address challenges that commonly affect us.

Drug policy as a global public policy is an exercise in an international public 'bad'. The negative externalities of criminalization are universal and non-excludable. They impact public health, security and development, and disproportionately hurt the poorest and most vulnerable countries and communities. The challenge in drug policy is not how to build a system of global governance and regulation, but how to deconstruct it.

Drug criminalization is a programmatic failure, but it is a *political* success in terms of other objectives and goals. These are distinct from the regulation of dangerous substances. It is a strategy for reinforcing structures of order and power, strengthening the coercive capacity of the state, embedding racial, gendered and socio-economic hierarchies, and recycling existing norms and prejudices.

A long historical lens demonstrates how commercial and political interests in the criminalization regime have accumulated. Path dependence, and the process of layering onto founding ideas and treaty agreements, has embedded a range of vested interests in the status quo. This ranges from pharmaceutical companies to private prison providers, defence contractors to therapeutic communities.

Bilateral and multilateral trade and security agreements are routinely leveraged through counternarcotics cooperation and assistance. For the US, the quest to control the international flow of narcotics by eliminating illicit drug supply at source overseas has positioned the country to influence the security, defence and trade arrangements of other countries. As such, drug policy has served a variety of other ends. Drug policy is bad policy, but it is good politics.

What is drug policy for? There is little evidence that it is about preventing public access to dangerous drugs or improving access to pain-relieving medicines. If it were, criminalization strategies and the UN drug treaties would have been jettisoned decades ago.

FURTHER READING

This list of readings is intended to be an accessible follow-up to some of the issues raised in the book and a guide to the sources used. Breaking with any rules of alphabet, the principal author recommended is Professor Dave Bewley-Taylor of the University of Swansea. A respected academic historian of international drug control and a founder and member of drug reform NGOs, Dave died of cancer at the end of 2024. This book is dedicated to his mentorship and friendship.

His classics include these:

Bewley-Taylor, D. (2002). *The United States and International Drug Control, 1909–1997*. Continuum.

Bewley-Taylor, D. (2012). *International Drug Control: Consensus Fractured*. Cambridge University Press.

GDPO publications

A key initiative of Dave's was the Global Drug Policy Observatory (GDPO) hosted at Swansea. This produced expert briefing reports that cover some of topics discussed in the book. For example, on darknet drug markets:

Afilipoaie, A. and Shortis, P. (2015). *From Dealer to Doorstep – How Drugs Are Sold on the Dark Net*. Available at: www.swansea.ac.uk/media/From-Dealer-to-Doorstep-%C3%A2%C2%80%C2%93-How-Drugs-Are-Sold-On-the-Dark-Net.pdf

Other relevant GDPO publications might include:

Buxton, J. (2015). *Drugs and Development: The Great Disconnect*. Available at: www.swansea.ac.uk/media/Drugs-and-Development-The-Great-Disconnect.pdf

Buxton, J., Bewley-Taylor, D. and Hallam, C. (2017). *Dealing with Synthetics: Time to Reframe the Narrative*. Available at: www.swansea.ac.uk/media/Dealing-with-Synthetics-Time-to-Reframe-the-Narrative.pdf

Csete, J. and Sánchez, C. (2013). *Telling the Story of Drugs in West Africa: The Newest Front in a Losing War?*. Available at: www.hr-dp.org/files/2014/04/15/GDPO_West_Africa_digital.pdf_FINAL_.pdf

Stengel, C. and Fleetwood, J. (2014). *Developing Drug Policy: Gender Matters*. Available at: www.swansea.ac.uk/media/Developing-drug-policy-gender-matters.pdf

Further notable writers

The work of Paul Gootenberg is of relevance for those with an interest in the cocaine trade:

Gootenberg, P. (2001). 'The rise and demise of coca and cocaine: as licit global "commodity chains", 1860–1950'. *Latin America and Global Trade conference*. Stanford University, 16–17 November. Social Science History Institute. Available at: http://hemi.nyu.edu/course-nyu/yuya/gootenberg.pdf

Jan Hoffman writes on the US opioid crisis:

Hoffman, J. (2021). 'Judge overturns Purdue Pharma's opioid settlement'. *New York Times*. Available at: www.nytimes.com/2021/12/16/health/purdue-pharma-opioid-settlement.html

Hoffman, J. (2022). 'Sacklers and Purdue Pharma reach new deal with States over opioids'. *New York Times*. Available at: www.nytimes.com/2022/03/03/health/sacklers-purdue-oxycontin-settlement.html

David Mansfield is a world-respected expert on Afghanistan. His writing on the country includes:

Mansfield, D. (2016). *A State Built on Sand: How Opium Undermined Afghanistan*, Hurst Publishers.

Mansfield, D. (2020). 'Trying to be all things to all people: alternative development in Afghanistan'. In: Buxton, J., Chinery-Hesse, M. and Tinasti, K. (eds) *Drug Policies and Development* (Conflict and Coexistence Series: International Development Policy, Volume 12), Brill | Nijhoff.

Mansfield, D. (2022). 'When the water runs out: the rise (and inevitable fall) of the deserts of Southwest Afghanistan and its impact on migration, poppy and stability'. *Afghanistan Research and Evaluation Unit (AREU)*. Available at: Afghanistan Research and Evaluation Unit | ReliefWeb

Mansfield, D. (2022). 'Methamphetamine production in Afghanistan'. *Alcis Storymaps*. Available at: https://storymaps.arcgis.com/stories/fc4f584da0274c25a6ce5f1064f05aee

The work of Alfred McCoy is frequently cited. His classics include:

McCoy, A. (1972). *The Politics of Heroin in Southeast Asia*. Harper & Row.

McCoy, A. (1991). *The Politics of Heroin: CIA Complicity in the Global Drug Trade*. Lawrence Hill Books.

McCoy, A. (2019). 'Searching for significance among drug lords and death squads: the covert netherworld as invisible incubator for illicit commerce'. *Journal of Illicit Economies and Development*, 1(1), pp. 9–22 (cited in Chapter 2).

Sources used in writing the book

Information for the final chapter on the outcomes of cannabis decriminalization includes:

Benfer, I.Z., Zahnow, R., Barratt, M.J., Maier, L., Winstock, A. and Ferris, J. (2018). 'The impact of drug policy liberalisation on willingness to seek help for problem drug use: a comparison of 20 countries'. *International Journal of Drug Policy*, 56, pp. 162–175.

Bradford, A.C. et al. (2018). 'Association between US state medical cannabis laws and opioid prescribing in the Medicare part D population'. *JAMA Internal Medicine*, 178(5), pp. 667–672.

O'Grady, M., Iverson, M., Suleiman, A. and Rhee, T. (2024). 'Is legalization of recreational cannabis associated with levels of use and cannabis use disorder among youth in the United States? A rapid systematic review'. *European Child & Adolescent Psychiatry*, pp. 701–723.

And on decriminalization contexts:

Decorte, T. and Pardal, M. (2020). 'Insights for the design of Cannabis Social Club regulation'. *Legalizing Cannabis*, pp. 409–426.

Eastwood, N., Fox, E. and Rosmarin, A. (2016). *A Quiet Revolution: Drug Decriminalisation Across the Globe*. Release.

Discussion of the suppression regime draws on:

Boister, N. (2002). 'Human rights protections in the suppression conventions.' *Human Rights Law Review*, 2(2), pp. 199–227.

On alternative development:

Brombacher, D. and David, S. (2020). 'From alternative development to development-oriented drug policies'. In: Buxton, J., Chinery-Hesse, M. and Tinasti, K. (eds). *Drug Policies and Development* (Conflict and Coexistence Series: International Development Policy, Volume 12). Brill | Nijhoff, pp. 64–78.

Renard, R. (2005). *Mainstreaming Alternative Development in Thailand, Laos PDR and Myanmar: A Process of Learning*. Available at: www.unodc.org/documents/alternative-development/Final_Published_version_Mainstreaming_AD.pdf

Other sources include:

Aldridge, J., et al. (2021). *Drugs in the Time of COVID: The UK Drug Market Response to Lockdown Restrictions*. Release (cited in Chapter 3).

CannStandard (2022). *Canadian Cannabis Market Summary – July 2022*. Available at: Canadian Cannabis Market Summary – July 2022 – CannStandard (cited in Chapter 5).

Caulkins, J.P. and Reuter, P. (2010). 'How drug enforcement affects drug prices'. *Crime and Justice*, 39(1), pp. 213–271.

Fazey, C.S.J. (2003). 'The Commission on Narcotic Drugs and the United Nations International Drug Control Programme: politics, policies and prospect for change', *International Journal of Drug Policy*, 14(2), pp. 155–169 (cited in Chapter 5).

Garland, D. (1990). *Punishment and Modern Society: A Study in Social Theory*. University of Chicago Press (cited in Chapter 3).

Garzón, J.C. and Rueda, A.M. (2020). 'Latin America and the Caribbean: complicity and legacy of a long war'. *Research Handbook on International Drug Policy*, Edward Elgar, p. 72 (cited in Chapter 4).

Leggett, T. (2002). *Rainbow Vice: The Drugs and Sex Industries in the New South Africa*. Zed Books.

Lupick, T. (2022). *Light Up the Night: America's Overdose Crisis and the Drug Users Fighting for Survival*. The New Press (cited in Chapter 5).

McAllister, W. (1999). *Drug Diplomacy in the Twentieth Century*. Routledge (cited in Chapter 4).

McCall, H., Adams, N., Mason, D. and Willis, J. (2015). 'What is chemsex and why does it matter?', *BMJ*. 3 November; 351:h5790. doi: 10.1136/bmj.h5790 (cited in Chapter 3).

Nutt, D.J. (2019). 'Psychedelic drugs – a new era in psychiatry?' *Dialogues in Clinical Neuroscience*, 21(2), pp. 139–147. Available at: https://pubmed.ncbi.nlm.nih.gov/31636488/

Nutt, D.J., King, L.A. and Phillips, L.D. (2010). 'Drug harms in the UK: a multicriteria decision analysis'. *The Lancet*, 376(9752), pp. 1558–1565 (cited in Chapter 2).

Parker, H. (2004). 'Heroin epidemics and social exclusion in the UK, 1980–2000'. *Heroin Addiction and The British System: Volume I Origins and Evolution*, p. 171.

Parker, H., Bury, C. and Egginton, R. (1998) *New Heroin Outbreaks Amongst Young People in England and Wales*, Home Office Police Research Group.

Pettus, K., De Lima, L., Maurer, M., et al. (2018). 'Ensuring and restoring balance on access to controlled substances for medical and scientific purposes: joint statement from palliative care organizations'. *Journal of Pain and Palliative Care Pharmacotherapy*, 32, pp. 124–128.

Sources of quotes used in the book

The quote in Chapter 2 from the *Pall Mall Gazette* on the Brussels Conference is taken from:

Cooper, N. (2018). 'Race, sovereignty, and free trade: arms trade regulation and humanitarian arms control in the age of empire'. *Journal of Global Security Studies*, 3(4), pp. 444–462.

Other sources of quotes include:

Dunlap, E., and Johnson, B.D. (1992). 'The setting for the crack era: macro forces, micro consequences

(1960–1992)'. *Journal of Psychoactive Drugs*, 24(4), pp. 307–321.

Harm Reduction International and reports can be found at: https://hri.global/

Transform Drug Policy Foundation https://transformdrugs.org/

International Network of People Who Use Drugs (INPUD). (2020). *Taking Back What's Ours! A Documented History of the Movement of People Who Use Drugs.* Available at: Taking Back What's Ours! A documented history of the movement of people who use drugs – (inpud.net)

Drug Science. *About Drug Science.* Available at: https://drugscience.org.uk/our-story/

Release: www.release.org.uk/

International Drug Policy Consortium: https://idpc.net/

TNI Amsterdam: www.tni.org/en

The EU Drugs Agency, previously the European Monitoring Centre for Drugs and Drug Addiction (EMCDDA): www.euda.europa.eu/index_en

Global Initiative against Transnational Organized Crime: https://globalinitiative.net/ (including Jason Eligh's report cited in Chapter 1: Eligh, J. (2021). *A Synthetic Age: The Evolution of Methamphetamine Markets in Eastern and South Africa*).

Also the following Global Commission on Drug Policy (GCDP) reports (cited in Chapter 1):

GCDP (2023). *HIV, Hepatitis and Drug Policy Reform.* Geneva.

GCDP (2024). *Criminal Justice Responses to Drugs: The Daily Impacts of Punitive Law Enforcement.* Geneva.

Official reports and the UN treaties

Organization of American States (OAS) (2013). *Report on the Drug Problem in the Americas.* Available at: www.cicad.oas.org/drogas/elinforme/informeDrogas2013/drugsDevelopment_ENG.pdf

Special Inspector General for Afghanistan Reconstruction (SIGAR). (2018). *Counternarcotics: Lessons from the US Experience in Afghanistan.* Available at: www.sigar.mil/Portals/147/Files/Reports/Lessons-Learned/SIGAR-18-52-LL-Executive-Summary.pdf

UK Independent Commission for Aid Impact. (2014). *DFID's Bilateral Support to Growth and Livelihoods in Afghanistan. Report 31.* ICAI.

UNAIDS. (2019). *Health, Rights and Drugs.* Available at: www.unaids.org/sites/default/files/media_asset/JC2954_UNAIDS_drugs_report_2019_en.pdf

United Nations. (1961). *Single Convention on Narcotic Drugs of 1961 as amended by the 1972 protocol.* Available at: www.unodc.org/pdf/convention_1961_en.pdf

United Nations. (1971). *Convention on Psychotropic Substances, 1971.* Available at: www.unodc.org/unodc/en/treaties/psychotropics.html

United Nations. (1988). *United Nations Convention Against Illicit Traffic in Narcotic Drugs and Psychotropic Substances, 1988.* Available at: www.unodc.org/pdf/convention_1988_en.pdf

United Nations General Assembly. (1998). *Action Plan on International Cooperation on the Eradication of Illicit Drug Crops and on Alternative Development.*

Villarreal, M. (2011). *ATPA Renewal: Background and Issues*. Congressional Research Service.

World Health Organization (WHO) (2004). *Effectiveness of Sterile Needle and Syringe Programming in Reducing HIV/AIDS Among Injecting Drug Users*.

WHO (2004). *Position Paper: Substitution Maintenance Therapy in the Management of Opioid Dependence and HIV/AIDS Prevention*.

WHO (2018). Information sheet on opioid overdose. Available at www.who.int/substance_abuse/information-sheet/en/

WHO (2019). *World Health Organization Model List of Essential Medicines, 21st List*.

Media articles

Some insightful short newspaper and web articles on trends and dynamics include:

Asmann, P. (2021). 'Methamphetamine taking over Mexico's domestic drug market'. *InSight Crime* (cited in Chapter 4).

Baum, D. (2016). 'Legalize it all'. *Harper's Magazine*. (cited in Chapter 4).

Doherty, J. (2023). 'The China-Mexico fentanyl pipeline: increasingly sophisticated and deadly'. *Guardian*.

Foderaro, L.W. (1988). 'Psychedelic drug called ecstasy gains popularity in Manhattan nightclubs'. *New York Times*.

Hickman, T. (2002). 'Heroin chic: the visual culture of narcotic addiction'. *Third Text*, 16(2), pp. 119–136.

International Cannabis Corp. (2018). 'International Cannabis adds cultivation licences in Bulgaria/Macedonia and Macedonia's only extraction licence'. *Globe News Wire*.

Schrad, M.L. (2022). 'The truth about prohibition'. *The Atlantic* (cited in Chapter 2). Available at: www.theatlantic.com/ideas/archive/2022/01/real-history-prohibition-global/620929/

Sommers, C. and Bernstein, E. (2020). 'Inside the FBI takedown of the mastermind behind website offering drugs, guns and murders for hire'. *CBS News*.

The book has been interwoven with quotes from this 2020 publication:

Buxton, J., Margo, G. and Burger, L. (eds) *The Impact of Global Drug Policy on Women: Shifting the Needle*. Emerald Publishing Ltd.

The US Congressional Research Service is a source of excellent reports including:

Beittel, J. and Rosen, L. (2017). *Colombia's Changing Approach to Drug Policy*. Congressional Research Service.

Congressional Research Service. (2013). *Central America Regional Security Initiative: Background and Policy Issues for Congress*. Congress. Available at: www.congress.gov/crs-product/R41731

From *The Economist*'s long catalogue of articles on drugs and drug policy, those used here include:

The Economist. (2007). 'Khun Sa (Chang Chi-fu), master of the heroin trade, died on October 26th, aged 73'.

The Economist. (2017). 'The Opium Wars still shape China's view of the West: Britain and China see each other through a narcotic haze'.

The Economist. (2018). 'Colombia's two anti-coca strategies are at war with each other'.
The Economist. (2019). 'A global revolution in attitudes towards cannabis is under way'.

Further reading on the book's themes

Race and racism in drug policy

Relevant books include:

Alexander, M. (2010). *The New Jim Crow: Mass Incarceration in the Age of Colorblindness*. The New Press.
Koram, K. (2019). *The War on Drugs and the Global Colour Line*. Pluto Press.

See also this report:

Eastwood, N., Shiner, M. and Bear, D. (2013). *The Numbers in Black and White: Ethnic Disparities in the Policing and Prosecution of Drug Offences in England and Wales*. Release.

Criminalization

Some of the important publications by human rights and development organizations as they have been drawn into debates on the outcomes and impacts of criminalization include:

Christian Aid (2019). *Peace, Illicit Drugs and the SDGs: A Development Gap*. Christian Aid.
Green, D. (2020). *Why are Illegal Drugs Still a Cinderella Issue in Development? (Looking at You CGD!)*. Oxfam.

Some follow-ups and cited reading on prisons, detention centres and criminal justice issues include:

Gotsch, K. and Basti, V. (2018). *Capitalizing on Mass Incarceration: U.S Growth in State Prisons*. The Sentencing Project.

Washington Office on Latin America (2016). *Women, Drug Policies, and Incarceration: A Guide for Policy Reform in Latin America and the Caribbean*. Available at: www.oas.org/es/cim/docs/womendrugsincarceration-en.pdf

On stigma, addiction and disease model debates:

Dehne, K., Khodakevich, L., Hamers, F. and Schwartländer, B. (1999). 'The HIV/AIDS epidemic in eastern Europe: recent patterns and trends and their implications for policy-making'. *AIDS*, 13(7), 741–749.

Granfield, R. and Reinarman, C. (2014). *Expanding Addiction: Critical Essays*. Routledge, Taylor & Francis Group.

Peele, S., Brodsky, A. and Arnold, M. (1992). *Truth About Addiction and Recovery*. Simon & Schuster.

On Latin America and the complexities of US relations

Isacson, A. (2012). 'Consolidating 'Consolidation': Colombia's 'security and development' zones await a civilian handoff, while Washington backs away from the concept'. Washington Office on Latin America.

Isacson, A. (2013). 'Time to abandon coca fumigation in Colombia'. Washington Office on Latin America.

Youngers, C. and Rosin, E. (2004). *Drugs and Democracy in Latin America: The Impact of US Policy*. Lynne Rienner.

FURTHER READING

Recommended general reading

Courtwright, D. (2002). *Forces of Habit: Drugs and the Making of the Modern World*. Harvard University Press.

DeGrandpre, R. (2006). *The Cult of Pharmacology: How America Became the World's Most Troubled Drug Culture*. Duke University Press.

Pollan, M. (2018). *How to Change Your Mind: What the New Science of Psychedelics Teaches Us About Consciousness, Dying, Addiction, Depression, and Transcendence*. Penguin.

Wainwright, T. (2016). *Narconomics: How to Run a Drug Cartel*. PublicAffairs (cited in Chapter 4).

INDEX

References to tables are in **bold**.

A
abstinence-based therapies 96–7
activism 153–6
addiction *see* treatment and support
Advisory Council on the Misuse of Drugs (ACMD), UK 37–8, 39, 143
advocacy 153–6
Afghanistan 31, 32, 112–13
  opium poppy cultivation 4, 5, 30, 83, 115, 117–18, 119, 130
Albania 31, 84, 152
alcohol 7, 8–12, 17–18, 38, 39, 41–5, 53
Alexander, Michelle 51
alternative development 107–12, 130
amphetamine 20, 25, 26, 40, 65, 79, 80, 89, 131
amphetamine-type substances (ATS) 13, 24–6, 79
Annual Report Questionnaire (ARQ) 20, 22
Anti-Saloon League 42, 44–5
Antigua and Barbuda 139, 140, 151
Antoniazzi, Tonia 144
Argentina 23, 146

Australia 4, 5, 10, 23–4, 25, 28
  cannabis 82, 138–9, 140
  decriminalization 137–40
  gangs 128
  heroin 74–5
  punitive turn 135
Azerbaijan 17

B
Bangkok Rules 17
Bangladesh 15, 25
Barbados 151
barbiturates 65, 79, 81
Baum, Dan 60–1
Belarus 85
Belgium 20
Belize 105, 139
Benzedrine 79, 80
benzodiazepines 38, 81, 88
Bewley-Taylor, Dave 161
Black, Carol 142
BMZ 111
Boister, Neil 59
Bolivia 16, 23, 84, 105, 112, 148
  coca cultivation and trade 30–1, 64, 77, 103, 104, 112, 114, 120
Brazil 16, 127, 129
Brownfield Doctrine, US 149–50, 163

INDEX

Brussels Conference Act 1890 53–4
Bulgaria 23, 84

C

Canada 10, 24, 32
  cannabis 137, 141, 152, 159
  decriminalization 138, 141, 145, 152, 159, 163
cannabis cultivation and trade
  cartels 123
  commercial model 159–61
  criminalization 31, 45, 51–2, 63, 82, 83, 103
  crop substitution 104
  decriminalization 137, 139, 140, 141, 151–2, 159–60
  exclusion and inequality 159–61
  pharmaceutical 151–2, 160
  profitability of 115
  scale of 108
cannabis use
  cannabis clubs 140–1
  classification of 40, 63, 143, 150–1
  decriminalization 137, 138–41, 143–5, 150–1, 156, 158–9
  historically 45, 51–2
  impact of criminalization 158–9
  impact of decriminalization 156
  international regulation 57
  medical use 143–5, 149, 151–2, 160
  scale of 22–3, 82, 156
  synthetic cannabinoids 27, 40
  and technology 86, 88
cartels 122–6

Central America Regional Security Initiative (CARSI) 105–6
chemsex 89
Chen, Adrian 87
Chile 23, 137, 140
China 25, 29, 32, 58, 85
  international regulation 55–6, 61–2
  migrants to US 49, 50–2
  open-door policy 85
  opium 48–9, 54, 58, 61–2
Christian Aid 108–9
civil society 152–6
classification/scheduling of substances
  cannabis 40, 63, 143, 150–1
  and clinical research 98–9
  and harm matrix 37–40
  League of Nations 57
  in UK 40, 143
  UN conventions 13–14, 39, 63–5, 78, 79, 80, 150–1
clinical research 13, 81, 98–9, 151–2
clinical use *see* medical use of drugs
Coca-Cola 46
coca cultivation and cocaine trade
  cartels and gangs 123, 125–6, 127
  and cocaine manufacture 121–2
  and criminalization 30–31, 64, 103
  and decriminalization 148
  during COVID-19 lockdown 128–9
  environmental impacts 116
  geographies of 119–22
  international regulation 56, 57
  medical supply 58, 64
  profitability of 114, 116

coca cultivation and cocaine trade (continued)
  scale of 30–1, 46–7, 114, 120–1
  seizures of 20
  substitution initiatives 104
  technological innovation 130
  value of 121
cocaine trade *see* coca cultivation and cocaine trade
cocaine use
  decriminalization 140
  harm matrix 38, 39
  historically 45–6, 51
  international marketplace 89
  price of 70
  and race and ethnicity 50, 51
  scale of 28, 76–7
coffee 8, 11, 114
Coke, Christopher 126
Colombia
  alternative development 112
  cannabis cultivation 152
  coca cultivation 30, 104, 116, 120–1
  cartels and gangs 123, 125, 128
  cocaine manufacture and trade 77, 120, 126, 128
  decriminalization 146
  fumigation of crops 107
  militarized anti-drug approach 105
  opium poppy cultivation 114, 119
colonialism 47–8, 49, 53–4, 55–6, 71, 72–3, 101–2
Commission on Narcotic Drugs (CND) 62, 133, 150, 163
COVID-19 lockdown 87–8, 128–9
crack cocaine 40, 76, 77

criminalization 6–33
  and authoritarianism 147
  coercive state and enforcement violence 14–19
  and deterrence 28–9, 91–9
  evaluation of strategy 20–33, 35–6, 164–5
  exceptionalism of drug control 35–41
  failure of 164–5
  globalization and drug-market convergence 83–91
  harms associated with 34–5
  impact of on drug use 72–82
  lack of credibility 92–3
  management of narcotic drug markets 12–14
  measuring success 20–1
  myths and reality 68–72
  post-war criminalization regime 59–62
  and risky behaviours 28–9
  scale of demand for drugs 21–8
  scale of supply 30–2
  state regulation of cigarettes and alcohol 9–12
  temperance or prohibition 8–9
  UN Conventions 63–6
  see also drug policy, historical evolution of; drug users; punishment and penalties; reform of drug policy; supply side
crop cultivation and control *see* supply side; *also see individual crops*
Czechia 23, 137, 140, **140**, 147

D

darknet 71, 86–7
Darwin, Charles 43
date rape drug 40, 91

INDEX

death penalty 14–15, 135
deaths, drug-related 7, 24, 28, 29, 38, 74, 94–6, 142, 143, 145
Decorte, Tom 140
decriminalization
   civil society 153–6
   conditions and mechanics for change 145–7
   context and contestation 156–9
   exclusion and inequality 159–64
   initiatives 134–5, 137–40
   multi-agency involvement 156–8
   positive results 156–9
   process of 138–9
   regulated supply and cannabis clubs 140–1
   shifts in international drug control 147–56
   threshold quantities 139–40
   UK drug policy 142–5
DeGrandpre, Richard 42
Dehne, Karl 85
demand side *see* drug users
Denham, Bryan 75
Denmark 97, 145, 152
deterrence, limits of 91–9
development approaches 107–12, 130
disease model of addiction 97–8
drug policy, historical evolution of 41–66
   change and continuity 62–6
   drug trade 45–9
   international alliance-building 52–5
   international structure of regulation 55–8
   post-war criminalization regime 59–62
   prohibition movement 41–5
   racialization of substance abuse 50–2
drug users 67–99
   and criminalization 68–72
   and deterrence 91–9
   evolving cultures 72–82
   and gender 89–90
   globalization and drug-market convergence 83–91
   international marketplace 88–91
   post-communism 83–5
   scale of use 21–8
   and technology 71, 86–8
   treatment and support 17–19, 93–9
   see also possession; supply side
dual use dilemma 1–2
Dunlap, E. 77
Duterte, Rodrigo 14–15

E

Economist, The 48, 152
Ecstasy 13, 27, 39, 40
Ecuador 23, 112, 127, 129
Ehrlichman, John 60–1
El Salvador 16, 105, 126, 127
Eli Lilly 81
Eligh, Jason 25–6
enforcement
   cigarettes and alcohol 10–12
   enforcement violence 14–19, 36
   and Hydra syndrome 124–6
   measuring success of 20–1, 36–7
   racist 93
   reforms 138–9
   and supply of drugs 69, 70, 72, 82, 106, 118–19, 132–3
   in UK 142
   see also criminalization; punishment and penalties

environmental impacts 116
ephedra cultivation 32
ephedrine 27, 31
eugenics 43–5, 53
European Monitoring Centre for Drugs and Drug Addiction (EMCDDA) 32

F

Fazey, Cindy 133–4
Fedotov, Yury 56
fentanyl 23–4, 32, 71
Forbes magazine 159
France 5, 23, 56, 82, 119, 123
Friedman, Milton 68
fumigation of crops 107

G

Galton, Francis 43–4
gangs 126–9
Garland, David 93
Garzón, Juan Carlos 125
Geneva Convention (1925) 57
Georgia 29
Germany
    drug use 23, 26, 46, 79, 137
    and international regulation 56, 58
    treatment and support 97, 145
GHB 40, 91
glamourizing drugs 75–6
Global Commission on Drug Policy (GCDP) 15, 155
Global Initiative against Transnational Organized Crime 25–6
global regulation
    change and continuity 62–6
    conferences 53, 54, 55–6
    conventions 56–7, 62–4
    exceptionalism of drug control 35–41
    international alliance-building 52–5
    international structure of regulation 55–8
    shifts in international drug control 147–56
    weak and corrupt states 71–2
    see also drug policy, historical evolution of; reform of drug policy; *United Nations entries*
Gootenberg, Paul 76
Green, Duncan 154
Guatemala 16, 105, 106

H

Hague International Opium Convention (1912) 56–7
harm categorisation *see* classification/scheduling of substances
Harm Reduction International 14, 18
harm reduction *see* treatment and support
Harper's Magazine 60–1
Harrison Narcotics Act 1914 (US) 51, 118
Hasina, Sheikh 15
Hearst, William Randolph 50
heroin manufacture and trade 27, 56, 58, 83, 123
    see also opium poppy cultivation
heroin use 3, 73–6, 85
    classification of 13–14, 63
    decriminalization 140
    harm matrix 38, 39
    international marketplace 89
    price 70
    scale of 25, 73–6
    treatment and support 94–6, 97

INDEX

Hippocrates 1
HIV/AIDS 29, 75, 85, 136–7, 138, 157
Hobson, Richmond P. 44–5, 54
Honduras 105, 106
Hong Kong 47, 48, 123
Human Rights-Based Approaches (HRBA) 11, 36, 94, 110
Hungary 23
Hydra syndrome 125–6

I

Iceland 10
illicit drug markets *see* supply side
imprisonment 15–16, 17, 93, 126–9, 135, 158
India 10, 31, 32
    opium poppy cultivation 5, 47, 48, 101–2
Indonesia 16, 25, 47, 58, 128
injecting drugs (PWID) 29, 89, 138, 145
Insite, Canada 138
International Narcotics Control Board (INCB) 62–3, 99, 133
International Network of People who Use Drugs (INPUD) 96–7, 154
international regulation *see* global regulation
internet trade 26–7, 71, 86–8, 124
Iran 14, 58, 64, 102–3, 117, 118
Italy 56, 123, 140

J

Jamaica 126, 128, 139, 140, 146, 151
James, I. Pierce 73–4
Japan 38, 58, 59–60, 79, 134
Java 47, 58
Jelsma, Martin 114–15, 161

Johnson, B.D. 77
Johnson, Boris 143, 144

K

kingpin approach 122–6, 129
Kyrgyzstan 17

L

Lancet, The 29, 33, 37–9
Laos 5, 15, 30, 104
League of Nations 56–8
Lebanon 31, 104, 160
legitimacy 92–3
Lesotho 25–6, 151, 152
LSD 39, 40, 65, 78, 79, 80, 162
Luxembourg 137

M

mafia 122–4
Malta 137, 140, 146, 163
Mansfield, David 115, 130
markets *see* supply side
Marx, Karl 52
McAllister, William 55, 101
McCall, Hannah 89
McCoy, Alfred 47–9, 126, 131
McKinley, William 54
MDMA 26, 39, 40, 65, 78, 79, 140, 162
Measham, Fiona 78
media 50–1, 52, 53–4, 146–7
medical use of drugs
    cannabis 143–5, 149, 151–2, 160
    coca and cocaine 58, 64
    and international regulation 57, 58, 59, 60, 63, 64, 66, 79
    pain relief 1–5, 33, 46, 66, 92, 98–9, 151
    psychedelics 162
    psychotropics 81–2
    synthetics 79, 80
    women 73, 81

Merriman, Anne 4
methadone 18, 59, 94–5, 97
methamphetamine 12–13, 27, 39, 89, 131
   scale of use 20, 25–6, 59–60, 79
   supply of 31–2
Mexico 31, 32
   cannabis 103, 123, 140, 160
   cartels and gangs 123, 125, 128
   coca and cocaine 125, 126, 128
   decriminalization 137, 140, 140
   militarized anti-drug approach 105
   opium poppy cultivation 30, 104, 118–19
militarized anti-drug approach 105–7, 110, 120
Misuse of Drugs Act 1971 (UK) 40, 142
Morales, Evo 148
Morocco 31, 104, 115, 160
morphine 2–4, 45–6, 63, 73, 123
Mujica, José 141
Multidisciplinary Association for the Study of Psychedelics (MAPS) 162
Myanmar 5, 25, 30, 102, 104, 117, 119, 131

N

'narcodiplomacy' 55, 101, 102
Netherlands 26, 38, 56, 97, 139
New York Times 51
New Zealand 10, 24, 25
nitrous oxide 143
novel psychoactive substances (NPS) 26–7, 31–2, 40
Nutt, David 37–9, 65, 143

O

Obama, Barack 126–7, 149–50
Office of the High Commissioner for Human Rights (OHCHR) 155
online drug markets 26–7, 71, 86–8, 124
Operation Condor 103
opiates (general) 1–5, 45
   international regulation of 56, 57, 59, 60, 70–1
   scale of use 23–4, 73
   see also individual opiates
opioids (general) 13, 89, 97, 138
   scale of use 23–4, 29, 83
   see also individual opioids
Opium Advisory Committee (OAC) 57
opium poppy cultivation and trade
   alternative development model 109
   geographic shifts 117–19
   international regulation of 47–58, 60, 61–2, 64, 70–1, 101–3
   medical supply 4–5, 64
   profitability of 114, 115
   scale of 30, 114
   substitution initiatives 104
   technological innovation 130
opium use
   historically 47–9, 51–2, 61–2
   impact of criminalization on 70
   medically 58
Opium Wars 48–9
Organization of American States (OAS) 93, 106, 108, 116
organized crime 122–5

INDEX

P

pain relief 1, 2–5, 33, 46, 66, 92, 98–9, 151
Paine, Adam 115
Pakistan 31, 104, 117, 118
Pall Mall Gazette 53–4
Pardal, Mafalda 140–1
Parker, Howard 75, 76
Pease, Joseph 52
Pemberton, Dr John 46
Pereira, Isabel 107, 116
Permanent Central Opium Board (PCOB) 57
Peru 23, 105, 112
  coca cultivation and trade 30–1, 46–7, 58, 77, 103, 104–5, 112, 116, 120–1
pharmaceuticals *see* medical use of drugs
Philip Morris International 11–12
Philippines 14–15, 16, 25, 47, 54
pleasure of drugs 92
Poland 26, 43, 83, 84, 152
poppy cultivation *see* opium poppy cultivation and trade
Portugal 23, 38, 136
  decriminalization 137, **140**, 146, 147, 152
possession 15
  decriminalization 137–40, 158, 161
  UK drug scheduling 40
  UN conventions 65–6
post-traumatic stress disorder (PTSD) 162–3
price/value of drugs 70, 121–2
prisons *see* imprisonment
prohibition movement 8–12, 41–5, 50–2, 56, 68–72
Prozac 81–2
pseudoephedrine 27, 31

psilocybin 162–3
psychedelic and hallucinogenic substances 162–3
psychoactive plants 27
psychotropics 81–2
public education campaigns 11–12, 157
Public Safety Canada 71
Pulitzer, Joseph 50
punishment and penalties 12, 14–15, 21, 93
  depenalization 138, 140–1, 157, 158
  imprisonment 15–16, 17, 93, 126–9, 135, 158
  punitive turn 135–6
  and threshold quantities 139–40
  UK drug policy 40, 142, 144
  UN conventions 13, 39, 64, 65–6
PWID (people who inject drugs) 29, 89, 136–7, 138, 145

R

race and ethnicity
  and alcohol 53–4
  and Chinese migrants 49, 50
  and enforcement 15, 93
  post-war criminalization 60–1
  prohibition movement 43–5
  and substance use imagery 50–2
Ramírez, Lucía 107, 116
Reagan, Ronald 104–5, 120, 122–3, 135, 163
reform of drug policy 132–65
  civil society 152–6
  conditions for change 142–7
  context and contestation 156–9
  decriminalization in practice 134–5, 137–40

reform of drug policy (continued)
   exclusion and inequality
      159–64
   positive results 156–9
   preventing spread of disease
      136–7
   regulated supply and cannabis
      clubs 140–1
   resistance to change 133
   shifts in international drug
      control 147–56
   within criminalization
      paradigm 134
Release 88
religion 8, 42, 43
risks of substance use 7, 8, 28–9,
   89, 136–7; *see also* deaths,
   drug-related
Ritzer, George 83
Roosevelt, Franklin D. 51–2
Roosevelt, Theodore 54
Rowntree, Joseph 42
Rueda, Ana María 125
Russia 17, 29, 38, 84, 85, 134

S

Saudi Arabia 14, 20
schedules *see* classification/
   scheduling of substances
Schrad, Mark 41
Scotland 28, 38, 145
selective serotonin reuptake
   inhibitors (SSRIs) 81–2, 162
Sen, Amartya 36
Seychelles 29
Shanghai conference (1909)
   55–6
Shinawatra, Thaksin 15
Shower Posse 126
Silk Road 86–7
Sino-British Ten Years Agreement
   (1907) 48–9, 58
Smith, Mickey 82

smoking (tobacco) 7, 8–12,
   17–18, 39
social club models 140–1
South Africa 26, 115, 128, 146,
   147, 151, 152
Soviet Union 61, 82–5
Spain 23, 28, 54, 128, 137, 140,
   147
speed 80
stakeholder participation 35–6,
   139
Stares, Paul 89
stigma 94, 138
supply side 100–31
   crop alternatives 104,
      107–10
   crop control 101–7
   and decriminalization
      140–1
   development approaches
      107–12, 130
   drug seizures 20–1
   gangs 126–9
   globalization and drug-market
      convergence 83–91
   importance of drug crops
      113–22
   mafias and cartels 122–6
   militarized anti-drug approach
      105–7, 110, 120
   scale of under criminalization
      30–2
   synthetic drugs 130–1
   and technology 71, 86–8, 124,
      129–30
   see also criminalization;
      decriminalization; drug
      users; *United Nations*
      entries
Sweden 128, 134
Switzerland 97, 136–7, 140, 145,
   146
synthetic cannabinoids 27, 40

INDEX

synthetic drugs 40
   evolving drug-use cultures 78–80
   scale of use and supply 22, 24–7, 31–2, 38, 59, 71, 78–80, 89, 130–1
   UN Convention on Psychotropic Substances (1971) 64–5, 78, 79, 80
   see also individual drugs

T

Tajikistan 17
Tanzania 96–7
technology 71, 86–8, 124, 129–30
temperance 12, 41–2
Thailand 15, 16, 25, 109, 131, 139
THC 65, 151–2
therapeutic use *see* medical use of drugs
threshold quantities 139–40
Tokyo Rules 17
trade agreements 102–3, 112
trafficking *see* supply side
tramadol 24, 32
tranquillizers 65, 79, 81
Travis, Trysh 90
treatment and support 17–19, 74, 93–9, 136–7, 138, 145, 157
Trump, Donald 163
Turkey 5, 58, 102–3, 117, 119, 123

U

Uganda 4, 26, 151
Ukraine 85
United Kingdom 5, 16, 28, 78, 162
   alternative development 112
   cannabis 23, 82, 143
   classification of substances 40
   harm matrix 37–9
   heroin 73–4, 75, 76
   opium economy 47–9, 58, 101–2
   race and alcohol 53–4
   reform of drug policy 142–5
   temperance 41–2
United Nations
   Annual Report Questionnaire (ARQ) 20, 22
   human security paradigm 110
   post-war criminalization regime 59–64
   reform of drug policy 150–1, 155
United Nations Convention against Illicit Traffic in Narcotic Drugs and Psychotropic Substances (1988) 62, 65–6, 69, 72, 135–6
United Nations Convention on Psychotropic Substances (1971) 26, 39, 62, 64–5, 78, 79, 80, 162
United Nations Development Programme (UNDP) 108, 155
United Nations General Assembly Special Session on Drugs (UNGASS) 107–8
United Nations Office on Drugs and Crime (UNODC) 20
   and drug use 16, 22, 25, 27, 28, 29, 37, 74, 90, 94
   and global regulation 56, 62
   illicit drug supply 30, 67, 77, 87, 114, 120
   pain management 99
   and reform 133
   and stigma 94

United Nations Single Convention on Narcotic Drugs (1961) 1–2, 39, 59, 60, 62–4, 72–3, 93, 100–1, 102, 149, 150–1
United Nations Rules for the Treatment of Women Prisoners and Non-custodial Measures for Women Offenders (2010) 17
United Nations Standard Minimum Rules for Non-custodial Measures (1990) 17
United Nations Universal Declaration on Human Rights (1948) 11
United States
 alternative development 111–12
 cannabis 103, 137, 140, 149, 159–60
 cocaine 28, 46, 76–7, 121
 critics of reform 163
 crop control 102–6, 111–12
 decriminalization 140, 146, 148–50, 152, 159–60, 163
 fentanyl and China 32
 gangs 126–7
 heroin 73, 74
 and immigration 43, 49
 international regulation 55–6
 mafias and cartels 122–5
 methamphetamine manufacture 31
 militarized anti-drug approach 105–7, 110, 120
 opioid use 24
 opium 52–3, 54, 56, 102–3, 118–19
 post-war criminalization regime 59–62
 power of 165
 prohibition 10, 41–5, 50–2
 punitive turn 135
 PWID (people who inject drugs) 29
 racialization of substance abuse imagery 50–2, 54, 60–1
 resistance to change 134
 as superpower in drug policy 55
 war veterans 162
 women and drugs 16, 19
Uruguay 11–12, 23, 137, 140, 141

V

Vice magazine 147
violence 14–15, 34–5, 105–7, 126–9

W

Wainwright, Tom 122, 130
Waly, Ghada 22
war veterans 73, 74, 162
wartime use of drugs 74, 79, 83, 102
Westermeyer, Joseph 70
Williams, Edward Huntington 51
Wired 87
women
 access to help and treatment 18–19
 and drug policy 90, 107, 116
 drug use 7, 73, 81, 89–90
 imprisonment 16–17
 as parents 17, 18–19, 98
World Health Organization (WHO) 33, 63, 78, 81

Z

zero tolerance approach 135–6

www.ingramcontent.com/pod-product-compliance
Lightning Source LLC
Chambersburg PA
CBHW020410080526
44584CB00014B/1258